THE LONELY VETERAN'S
GUIDE TO COMPANIONSHIP

Living Out

Gay and Lesbian Autobiographies

David Bergman, Joan Larkin, and Raphael Kadushin,
Founding Editors

THE LONELY VETERAN'S GUIDE TO COMPANIONSHIP

Bronson Lemer

THE UNIVERSITY OF WISCONSIN PRESS

The University of Wisconsin Press
728 State Street, Suite 443
Madison, Wisconsin 53706
uwpress.wisc.edu

Printed in the United States of America
This book may be available in a digital edition.

Library of Congress Cataloging-in-Publication Data
Names: Lemer, Bronson, author.
Title: The lonely veteran's guide to companionship / Bronson Lemer.
Other titles: Living out.
Description: Madison, Wisconsin : University of Wisconsin Press, 2025. |
Series: Living out: gay and lesbian autobiographies
Identifiers: LCCN 2024032829 | ISBN 9780299350741 (paperback)
Subjects: LCSH: Lemer, Bronson. | Gay men—United States—Biography. |
Gay veterans—United States—Biography.
Classification: LCC HQ75.8.L46 A3 2025 | DDC 306.76/62092
[B]—dc23/eng/20241122
LC record available at https://lccn.loc.gov/2024032829

for Matt

A good companion shortens the longest road.

—*Kurdish proverb*

Contents

THE LONELY VETERAN'S
GUIDE TO COMPANIONSHIP

Gumshoe

I used to have an older sister. I guess *have* might not be the right word here, since she was never really mine. She was born one day in July 1979, but died the same day, not living long enough to take on the role of older sister. It is probably more appropriate to say that my parents lost a daughter a little over a year before I was born, but that feels so cold and impersonal. Like she was an ottoman or a rottweiler that had up and disappeared.

I didn't know much about this sister growing up. No one ever talked about her. There were no photos of her. No monogrammed onesies or pink blankets stashed away in a closet somewhere. No birthday marked on the calendar by our telephone. When my parents did talk about this sister, it was almost as if they were teasing my siblings and me by dropping information they knew would make us curious and then walking away before we could ask any questions.

"Did you know we had a baby before you?" my father asked the first time he brought her up.

I set the *Goosebumps* book I was reading in my lap and looked at him sideways, annoyed by a question I knew my father knew the answer to. I was eleven, the oldest of my father's six living children, a title I took seriously because it made me feel important. It came with authority and responsibility and power, and I liked at least two of those things. I'd been led to believe that being the oldest child meant something by all the movies and television shows and books where firstborns bossed around their siblings and ruled kingdoms handed down to them. It was such a privileged position, and, being from a working-class family, I cherished the rare opportunities when I got to lord myself over others, even if it was just my five siblings.

After hearing my father's question, my brain kept looping the *before you* part over and over in my head. *Before* me? Before *me? There was someone before me?* I felt a hot wave of jealousy wash over me. One moment I was the oldest; the next moment there was someone new on the scene—this ghostly sister circling the room with her new title, relegating me to second in line. It didn't really matter that this new sister was no longer alive. It was the principle of the matter that bothered me. I was the oldest *living* child in my family, but, technically, I wasn't the oldest. That title had been taken away by the mere mention of an older sister, and that stung. It felt as if my father had snuck in and stolen something from me. *No one wants to be second*, I thought. *Second is the first loser.*

"What happened to her?" I asked after my initial burst of jealousy had faded.

I was too young to realize how painful it can be to lose *any* child, especially your first one. Only years later did I even start to understand this rare moment of vulnerability from my father—standing before me, letting me in on this pain—and wonder what I could do to get him to feel that vulnerable with me again.

"She died," he said, and then he turned away from me and stared out our front window, possibly lost in thoughts of what might have been.

2.

That fall, I was at the library book fair, perusing all the books laid out on the tables, the ones we could buy and take home with us and keep, when one book caught my eye. On the cover was a woman in a red trench coat and black fedora, holding a briefcase. She was mid-stride, as if the artist had captured her in the middle of a caper. I knew this woman. She was the same woman I'd chased in the computer games I used to play before school. She *always* wore that red trench coat with the popped collar and the wide-brimmed fedora that shaded half her face. She was Carmen Sandiego.

I took the book into my hands. *YOU ARE THE DETECTIVE*, it read across the book's cover. I flipped the book over. *HELP CAPTURE CARMEN SANDIEGO AND HER VILE BAND OF BAD GUYS!* It was the book version of the computer game *Where in the World Is Carmen Sandiego?*, with numbered passages like the ones in the *Choose Your Own Adventure* books I loved so much. The reader played the role of a detective tasked with flying around the world, interviewing bystanders, and collecting clues in order to arrest Carmen and her gang. I had to have it.

When I got home, I took the book to my room to start the first case. I sat on the floor next to my bed and turned to the briefing on the first page. *Congratulations, you've been hired as a rookie detective for the Acme Detective Agency.* I felt a surge of excitement ripple through my body. *Your goal is to outsmart Carmen Sandiego and her gang by solving the cases in this book.* Carmen and her gang stole four "treasures" from four different countries, I read in the briefing, and if I solved the cases and recaptured the treasures in a timely manner, I would receive a promotion.

The stolen treasures were printed on cards in the middle of the book. I tore the cards out and examined each one. There was the torch from the Statue of Liberty (just the torch, not the entire monument), a mountain gorilla stolen from Uganda, and a Stradivarius violin, which—according to the information printed on the back of the card—was created by an Italian instrument maker who created a "secret varnish" that gave his violins a distinct sound, a detail that was proved false many years later. The final case in the book was the most unbelievable, the one that most reminded me of the computer game: the theft of the Great Wall of China. This was part of the humor of chasing Carmen Sandiego. She often stole unusual or impossible things. All the salt from the Dead Sea. The secret recipe for kimchi. Plans to the sultan's harem. I appreciated the magnitude of Carmen's capers. She stole *anything* she wanted, big or small, living or inanimate, mobile or static. Ancient artifacts, symbolic animals, even stone walls that stretched for thousands of miles. Nothing was off-limits.

Carmen wasn't afraid to take what she wanted, and reading about the treasures she and her gang stole made me believe I could pursue the

answers to my own mysteries, like the disappearance of my favorite
cap gun and what had happened to this dead older sister.

3.

There was a certain rhythm to chasing Carmen and her gang, one I
found exciting. When reading the books, I would fly to a city by turning to a certain numbered passage and then reading some factoid
about the place I'd landed in (Beijing was once made up of a series of
smaller, walled-in cities; New York City was the capital of the United
States from 1785 to 1790; half a million pilgrims visit the holy city of
Mecca, Saudi Arabia, every year). The factoids were brief and memorable and didn't bore me like the information I read in my school history
books. Then, a local contact would appear and provide information
on three witnesses who had seen the thief I were chasing. These witnesses were local characters who often matched up with the locations—
like the used-camel salesman in Saudi Arabia or the Māori warrior in
New Zealand or Lisa from Pisa. When I interviewed the witnesses,
they said things like *He wanted an article on the migratory patterns of wild
yak* and *She wanted to kill a mockingbird*. Sometimes they gave vital information about where the suspect went or what the suspect looked
like, and I'd jot these clues down in my notebook. Other times they
brushed me off and turned back to their work without telling me much
of anything.

Reading those books, I learned to luxuriate in the pleasures of an
active life. We were meant to move around this world, to explore, to
attain knowledge, to live with meaning and purpose. Not only was I
led to believe that seeing the world was possible but going through the
motions of chasing someone helped me understand what it would take
for me to get what I wanted. Tracking Carmen and her gang was never
easy; there was always a series of motions you had to go through to
figure out the cases in the books. But, if you put in the time going
through those motions, it would all pay off in the end.

If I had to pinpoint the thing that first triggered my eventual wanderlust—my own need to explore—chasing Carmen and her gang in these
books would be it. Curled up on the floor of my childhood bedroom,

I felt important, needed, like I wasn't just some lonely kid longing to escape the North Dakota farm he was growing up on. My father may have taken something away from me when he told me about my older sister, but so much more was possible. There was a whole world, places I'd read about and pictured in my mind, and if I paid attention and asked the right questions and collected the appropriate information, I could experience those places. I could reach out and touch the ancient stones of an old wall, feel the air rush against my face as I pushed my way up the wall's steep incline, look up to see the wall snake through the surrounding hills.

4.

You land in North Dakota, a place of prairies and farmland. In the summer, there are fields of swaying wheat and towering cornstalks. In the fall, the fields are littered with hay bales of straw or alfalfa. But you haven't arrived in summer or fall. It is winter here, and the fields are covered in a blanket of never-ending snow. You look out and can see snow all the way to the horizon. You shiver and pop up the collar of your trench coat.

You trudge through the snow to a local farm and stand at the end of a long driveway, staring up at a farmhouse. You watch a man leave the house and walk across the yard to a barn. He disappears inside. Through the large window on the farmhouse, you see a woman watching the man. She is smiling. Then, you feel a tap on your shoulder and turn to find a little girl pulling a sled. She is maybe five years old, bundled up in a thick coat, hat, and mittens. You smile at her, but before you can ask her anything, she hands you a note with a list of witnesses and locations to investigate. You hold the note in your shivering hands and read the list. When you look up to thank the girl, she is gone.

If you want to talk to:

Your father—go to 1.
The house cleaner who also claims to be a spiritual medium—go to 10.
Your mother—go to 7.

If you want to investigate:

Your childhood bedroom—go to 5.
A college computer lab from the 1990s—go to 9.
The Catholic graveyard in your hometown—go to 12.

5.

Even with this new motivation to act and learn, I wasn't especially brave when it came to talking to adults. I was a kid who lived in his head, the one with his nose in a book and all these imaginary worlds created from the stories I had read. In my imagination, I could easily approach any adult and probe them for information. But, in reality, I often froze up and stammered when talking to adults. I was often afraid of asking the wrong thing or making people upset or saying something stupid. I once admitted to loving the song "I Feel Lucky" by Mary Chapin Carpenter, a country tune I thought was just about having luck on your side but was really about hooking up with a bunch of men, and this made my high-school aged cousin laugh and shake his head and say something about understanding that song when I was older (I did, and I love that song even more now).

While I worked up the courage to ask about my dead sister, I created a list of witnesses who probably knew something about her. My father was at the top of my list. I knew that if I caught him at just the right moment, he would tell me more. He was strange like that. He wasn't especially open about his feelings or other information about his life, but every now and then he'd get nostalgic and tell you some story from his past or other information you didn't know. The trick was figuring out the chemistry of those moments, how to manufacture another situation where he would open up. But, as with any good trick, the solution was difficult to decipher.

My three grandparents surely knew something about my dead sister, but asking them questions proved difficult. Grandma Mildred was stern and matter of fact. I often found it difficult approaching her with *any* type of question, especially a question about a dead older sister. I was certain that if I asked her, she'd simply brush it off. My sole living grandfather—Grandpa Dennis—had slurred speech from his dentures, so I often couldn't understand much of what he said. Grandma Beatrice, my father's mother, was kind yet moody, and if I didn't catch her at the right moment—same as with her son—I risked getting scolded or told to mind my own business. Asking any of them was risky because it might get back to my parents that I was poking around, asking questions I had no business asking, and I wasn't sure what would happen then.

My five siblings were also on my list of witnesses, but I figured that, as the oldest child in the family, if I didn't know anything about my dead sister, they probably didn't know anything either. Still, I added them to my list because it was possible that my parents or grandparents or someone else had mentioned something—just like my father had to me—and I thought asking them about our dead sister may warrant some surprising information.

The person I felt most comfortable asking about my dead sister was my mother, but, as with my father, I had to tread lightly. She had yet to say anything about my sister to me, so I figured that broaching the topic would be difficult. She might cry or get upset if I asked her, and I never wanted to make my mother cry. When my siblings joked that I was my mother's favorite, she didn't shake her head and deny it. Instead, she'd smile at me and wink. There was no denying that we had a special bond, one partially created by my sister's death and the fact that I was my mother's first child to survive childbirth, and I didn't want to jeopardize our relationship by dredging up something upsetting like a dead daughter. So, I stayed quiet and watched her from afar. I followed her around the house and across the farm, thinking that maybe she'd just blurt something out, maybe another secret or a piece of information I could add to my notebook of clues.

When I got bored with tracking my mother, I went to my room and pulled the milk crates out from under the bed. The crates held clues to my mother's life before my father, from a time when my mother was young and single and unencumbered. I flipped through a crate full of records—Bread and the Eagles and the Oak Ridge Boys. I found a photo album of my mother when she was thin and had beautiful, wavy hair.

I saw my mother happy and smiling and laughing with her friends. In one photo, my mother hung from a flying trolley car while my god-mother, Jane, and another woman laughed at her. It was clearly a doc-tored photo from a tourist destination, but I didn't know that then. As a child, I just stared at the photo and picked apart the pieces in order to make meaning out of the whole. The smiles. The clouds surrounding the trolley. The look on my mother's face. I was a gumshoe in training, so all these details told me something. I just wasn't sure what that was.

6.

Whenever I got a new *Carmen Sandiego* book (there are eight books in the series), I spent a few minutes just looking over the suspects' names and cartoon images. The suspects were operatives for Carmen's Vil-lains' International League of Evil (or V.I.L.E for short), each with their own evildoer name. There was Auntie Bellum, a proper southern belle with a straw hat and fan; Chuck Roast, an overweight butcher with a tiny mustache, a bowtie, and a meat cleaver; Justin Case, a black-haired lawyer-type with a wide grin and a toothpick. As I looked them over, I mouthed their names to myself and chuckled when I got the puns used for many of the names. Then, I carefully tore the cards along the perforated line and removed them from the book. On the back of each card was pertinent information for solving the cases—hair color, eye color, occupation, favorite food, and weakness. I took a few min-utes to read through this information. Auntie Bellum (whose full name was Eulalie "Auntie" Bellum) was a "professional southern" and liked shoofly pie (whatever that was). Ernest Endeavor—who looked a little like one of my teachers with his sweater-vest, wire-rim glasses, and blonde puff of hair—sold cellos door-to-door. Kari Meback's occu-pation was "cat burglar." I didn't know what that was—*Did she steal cats?*—so I just shrugged and moved on.

Carmen Sandiego wasn't always one of the suspects, but in the first book she was. On her suspect card, she wore her signature red trench coat, a necklace of scarlet jewels, and a gray snap-brim fedora shading her eyes. I knew I wasn't supposed to like her, but I did. I stared at her image and imagined the kind of mysterious life she lived, running from place to place, seeing the world, never letting anyone get too close. There was something intriguing about that life, something I couldn't help admiring. I wanted a life like that, one of adventure and intrigue and a little bit of mischief.

I kept the suspect cards from the books in a box under my bed, and periodically I'd take them out, rifle through the deck, and imagine what it would be like to be a part of Carmen's band of misfit operatives with goofy names and weird occupations. I gave myself a silly name (Mark Myword), an occupation (I wanted to be an architect around this time), and a favorite food (chocolate). It felt like a betrayal to pretend I was a V.I.L.E. criminal, but I justified it by thinking of myself as a double agent working both for the Acme Detective Agency and V.I.L.E. I'd gather information from the inside. That's what a good gumshoe would do.

In the Case of the Great Wall of China, Carmen ends up being the culprit, even though witnesses kept mentioning a "blue-eyed woman" and her suspect card listed her eyes as being brown. *It can't be Carmen*, I thought, flipping between the witness statements and Carmen's suspect card. *The suspect card lists her eyes as brown.* This discrepancy between the color of Carmen's eyes and those of the suspect excited me. *The writer of the book must have done this on purpose*, I thought, *to throw off unworthy gumshoes.* Only the best gumshoes—the ones who paid attention to the details and asked the right questions—would be able to figure this out.

7.

We were in our van—my mother behind the wheel and all five of my siblings and me in the back—headed back to the farm. Outside it was a beautiful summer day. The sun was bright. There was a slight breeze blowing through the tall grasses in the ditch. Someone was baling hay in one of the fields.

I was in the way-back of the van, looking out the window, when my mother—out of nowhere and to none of us kids in particular—said, "Today would have been your older sister's birthday."

This should have been where I pounced. I'd been watching my mother for months, waiting for more clues, following my mother around the house, watching her when she got emotional, hoping she would let me in on the details about my older sister, and here she was blurting out information no one had asked for. I should have followed up with one of the dozens of questions I'd put together in my head. *What did she look like? What was her name? Was dad there when she was born?* But I didn't. I couldn't. I looked at my mother from the back of the van, and, instead of asking about my sister, I started singing "Happy Birthday to You."

I didn't make it to the part where you are supposed to fill in the person's name (if I had, what would I have said? Older Sister? Dead Sister? I didn't know if she had even been given a name.). Just after the second line of the song, my mother yelled "Stop!" suddenly, and the van got very quiet. I looked down at my hands, waiting for somebody to say something, anything to break the tension. I wasn't sure what I had done wrong. We always sang when it was someone's birthday.

We sat in silence for a few moments and then, slowly, all the sounds started coming back. First the gravel under the tires. Then the gentle wind. Finally, the sound of my mother softly crying.

8.

Sometimes, if my detective work got sloppy or if I got cocky thinking I knew all the answers, I wouldn't even interview all the witnesses. I'd interview one witness and then jump to one of the three locations. Often, when I did this, I got a dead end, a fake trail. I'd find that the place I'd jumped to was deserted, that I'd been tricked by Carmen's gang and had fallen off the trail of my suspect. The dead ends had phrases like *It's very foggy, and a lot of the fog is inside your head* or *That oily crook has given you the slip!*

Once, when I got to one of these dead ends, a woman appeared out of the crowd and handed me a note with a poem written on it:

Roses are red, violets are blue,
Boy, have I made a sucker out of you.
You've certainly come to just the wrong place,
So, head back to where you came from, and you'd better make haste.

Boy. Sucker. You. I *was* a sucker who liked to believe he was wiser than he really was. Chasing Carmen and her gang was just a game, but sometimes those dead ends brought up this deeper fear that I'd never be enough, that I'd never be smart enough or strong enough or quick enough to lead the kind of life I wanted to live. *What would I do then?*

I didn't let my mind linger on these thoughts when I was a kid, but later, in my teens and twenties, I'd obsess over this fear. I'd let the fear consume the quiet moments between dead-end jobs and lackluster boyfriends. *Maybe I just didn't have what it took to have the life I wanted. Maybe I never would.*

9.

During my first year of college, I came across a study that focused on gay men with older brothers, and thoughts of my older sister came flooding back after years of lying dormant. The study concluded that men are more likely to be gay if a male child occupied the mother's womb before them, with some discussion about the mother's body recognizing successive male children as foreign and developing antibodies that entered the brains of these male children.

I found the whole study fascinating. The womb protecting the mother. The threatening nature of younger brothers. Antibodies entering the brains of fetuses. It all seemed like something from a science-fiction novel. I hadn't yet come to terms with my sexuality, so I read the study over and over, hoping it would provide answers, but all the study really did was make me long for my older sister.

Reading the study uncovered a desire I'd never before acknowledged: a yearning for a mentor. I liked being an older brother to my siblings, but there were times when I longed for an older sibling myself, someone to mentor me on the ins and outs of life, to introduce me to art and literature and music, to steer me away from destructive paths, to listen as I questioned my own same-sex desires. I wanted this kind of supportive, intimate relationship I'd always imagined having an older sibling was like. I wanted someone or something to tether myself to, a guiding star to steer me in the right direction. In some ways, I found this type of relationship with the men I dated, most of whom were older than I was. But that wasn't the same. These men were temporary, fleeting, proxies for the mentorlike older sister I'd created in my head. When I broke up with these men, I was left with an even deeper longing for someone to guide me in the right direction. In this way, each breakup brought me back to my older sister.

I saved the study, and from time to time I would take it out and reread it, thinking about my sister and what gets handed down and my failed search for answers when I was younger. Then I'd file the study away with other mementos and forget about my sister again. This went on for years. Over and over and over. My older sister would pop into my head, I'd briefly think about her, then she'd be whisked away by another thought, another memory, another task that took precedence over finding out what happened to her. In this way, The Case of the Dead Sister went cold for years.

10.

When I was thirty-five, I received a text message from the woman who periodically cleaned my house.

"Sometimes weird things happen to me," the woman wrote. "I hear/see things. I ignore it a lot, but sometimes it helps me to talk about it so it will stop."

I paused reading the message and wondered where it was headed.

"When I clean your house," the woman continued, "I hear a small child saying, 'He's my brother' over and over and over."

It's her, I thought. After all these years of floating into and out of my life, she was finally reaching out to let me know she was still there. I felt the hairs on my arm prickle after reading the message. I'd always been skeptical of ghosts and spirits, but I'd also been waiting for another clue about my sister, something to help me pick up the case again and try to figure out the answers to the questions I'd long since abandoned.

I spent a lot of time trying to *feel* my sister's spirit after reading the house cleaner's message. I stepped cautiously around my house, pausing to listen for my sister in my office, at the top of the stairs, in the middle of the open basement. I stood stock-still and cocked my head to the side, the way I did when my father first told me about my older sister. I didn't really need to hear what the house cleaner had heard in my house. It was enough just knowing that she was there, nearby, keeping watch, waiting for me to come chase after her again.

11.

I bought all eight books in the *You Are the Detective* series and captured Carmen three times. In *Where in the World Is Carmen Sandiego?*, I tracked her to Waikiki Beach, where she was suntanning. When I tossed her a towel, she caught it and then darted off into the ocean, where police officers rose up off surfboards to apprehend her.

"You win this time," Carmen snarled. "But next time—watch out!"

In *Where in Space Is Carmen Sandiego?*, Carmen stole Halley's Comet. I tracked her across the cosmos—from Saturn to an asteroid group called "Trojans and Greeks" to Mercury and Jupiter. I eventually captured her on Mars. In *Where in America's Past Is Carmen Sandiego?*, Carmen nabbed "Old New York City." I tracked her to a plantation in Hawaii, where she toppled a trailer of pineapples onto me and said, "Hah, gumshoe. I've given you the slip again."

I loved it when she called me gumshoe.

I tackled her, put her in handcuffs, and sent her off to jail. But Carmen never stayed captured for very long. She always broke out and rallied her gang for another series of heists.

There was something enjoyable about imagining Carmen this way— always on the move, forever elusive, out there waiting for me to come and catch her. When I chased Carmen and her gang, I was always in motion, moving from country to country, from witness to witness, from one choice to the next, and there was a part of me that never wanted the cases to end. I wanted to forever be chasing Carmen and her gang because that meant that I was doing something right. I was making the right choices and living the kind of life I'd always dreamed about. I would later come to admire this constant wanderlust when I read about the lives of Ernest Hemingway and Jack Kerouac and James Baldwin, and I would emulate it with my own life choices during my twenties and early thirties. I found comfort in this constant movement, in the idea that there was always something novel and thrilling on the horizon. I wanted to hold onto this feeling, to capture how it felt to be lured by the unknown, the incomplete, the unsolved. To chase something I knew could never truly be pinned down.

12.

I was at a baseball game with my husband when I received a text from my sister-in-law Courtney asking why no one had ever told her about my older sister.

"Because we never talked about her," I texted back. "When we were kids, we were conditioned to never bring her up."

I didn't tell her about my father casually mentioning my older sister from time to time or the incident in our family's van when I made my mother cry. She didn't need to know all the ways my parents avoided talking about their first child. Instead, I asked how she found out. She replied with a picture of my sister's gravestone.

My sister is buried in a Catholic cemetery in my hometown, along the southern edge with all the other children and babies. She doesn't have a name, although my parents may have chosen one and never told me. Her grave marker simply says BABY GIRL LEMER, the Y and Ls faded from weather and age.

I have one memory of visiting my sister's grave as a child. It was spring. The sun was out. The sky was very blue. Beyond the graveyard, seedlings were beginning to emerge in the open field. I remembered wandering the length of the graveyard—maybe an average city block—and then turning and seeing my parents standing along the edge of the cemetery looking down, where my sister's grave must have been. I turned away from them and looked out into the field, not really thinking about death but also not *not* thinking about it. When I turned back to look at my parents, they were walking back to the car.

After the house cleaner's message reinvigorated my search, I visited my sister's grave for the first time as an adult. I used my memory of visiting her grave as a child to guide me to where I thought she was buried. I placed a rose on her grave and lingered for a few minutes, hoping something would happen, that I would find more clues about her. But nothing happened. I didn't find any answers there. It wasn't a dead end like in the Carmen Sandiego books either. It was simply the final checkpoint—the last place the suspect landed before they were captured. Looking at my sister's gravestone, I knew what I had to do. I had to ask my parents directly about my sister.

A few months later, my parents visited me in St. Paul. We were sitting on my back patio, watching the birds chattering in the scraggly pines in my yard. I was nervous because I knew that I had to ask them about my older sister. I wasn't sure what I was expecting to get from them, but I needed to at least ask about my sister, to get some kind of closure after dredging up her memory again.

"I went to visit Baby Girl Lemer," I said during a lull in our conversation.

At first, they didn't say anything. Then my father chimed in.

"She would have been thirty-nine this year."

"July 16," my mother added.

This was new information. I never knew the exact day of my sister's birth and death. I knew that my parents were twenty-three and twenty-four years old when my sister died. Newly married. Just starting to build a life together. My sister-in-law once asked my mother about my older sister, and my mother told her that the doctor had known right away that something was wrong because my sister wasn't moving after she was born. She was still. My mother feared that my sister's death meant that she wouldn't be able to have any children. If that fear had persisted and prevented my parents from trying to have more children, I would have never been born.

"I dug her grave myself," my father said.

My parents were silent after this. They stared at the twittering birds and the flowers in the garden and the plane climbing into the sky overhead. They didn't have anything else to say.

Sitting in that silence, I thought about what they'd said and whether this new information was enough to satisfy the mystery of my older sister that I'd set out to solve when I was a child. I wasn't sure it was. But I also knew that I didn't have a right to probe my parents any further, to ask them to tell me more about their pain. I'd finally asked them about my sister's death. I'd let them know that I was thinking

18

about them and what they had gone through and why it was so difficult for them to talk about her. I didn't understand any of that when I was growing up, but I did as an adult, and that was enough. It was enough to simply acknowledge what they'd gone through and why it was so difficult for them to talk about it. These real-life mysteries weren't as neat and tidy as the ones in the Carmen Sandiego books.

"Great work," the Chief would say in the books when gumshoes called after solving a case. "Now add up those travel points and head for the score chart at the back of the book to see if you've earned a promotion!"

I was never good at keeping track of my travel points when I traveled from passage to passage in the books, so when it came time to see if I had gotten a promotion, I always imagined I had done well enough to be promoted to "super-sleuth" or at least "private eye." But the promotion wasn't important. I wasn't after a new title. I was fine with just being called gumshoe.

Withers

The judge was asking me about my pony, and, instead of listening to him, I stared at his bolo tie and imagined that the two cords were snakes, their heads levitating from his chest every time a breeze blew through the barn.

"How do you measure the height of a horse?" the judge asked.

I stared back at him blankly. I had no idea. I was standing in my size-3 cowboy boots, a green, four-leaf clover badge safety-pinned over my heart, my right forearm and wrist in a plaster cast, hanging at my side. I shifted awkwardly from foot to foot because I was worried about screwing up my first 4-H interview. It was June 1989, the summer after third grade, a month after I slid on the wet grass and broke my right arm, and I was presenting my Welsh pony named Blackie as part of the 4-H Horsemanship Program at the Wells County Fair in North Dakota. The leader of our 4-H club had encouraged my mother to enter Blackie and me in a few of the horsemanship contests—to give me practice in showing my pony—so my mother signed us up for the easy categories, like showmanship, western horsemanship, and the costume contest. This category—with the judge—was the interview portion of the program, where men in cowboy hats and bolo ties asked 4-Hers trick questions about their animals.

The judge bent over, placed his hands on his knees, and looked me in the eyes. The bolo-tie snakes leaned away from his shirt and hissed.

"Hands," the judge said, answering his own question. "You measure horses and ponies in hands."

Blackie was tied up outside his stall for the interview, and when the judge said this, I first looked at Blackie and then down at my own hands. I felt bad because there was so much I didn't know about my pony. I didn't know where he came from, who his parents were, if he had siblings. I didn't know how to make him canter, that weird medium speed between slow trot and sprinting gallop. I didn't know what to do if, while in the arena during one of the fair competitions, he suddenly bucked back, raised his front legs, and took off galloping for the gate. I certainly didn't know what to do if Blackie got away, if he pulled the reins free from my hand while I was walking him around the horse barn and raced off through the fairgrounds, knocking over children and carnies along the way.

I thought Blackie was just an ordinary pony, like all the other ponies. Basic just like me.

The judge stood up straight. The snakes wrapped themselves around each other. Slowly, he stepped up next to Blackie. He patted Blackie on the nose a few times, cooed something in his deep voice, and then ran his palm back and forth along Blackie's neck.

"Here," the judge said, motioning at me. "Stand here and hold your pony."

I stepped over and grabbed the halter, making sure to stand slightly off to Blackie's side because my mother told me to never ever stand directly in front of a horse or a pony. *That is how you get trampled*, she'd said.

I watched as the judge ran his hand from Blackie's neck all the way down Blackie's front leg. He slowly lowered himself so that he was crouching next to Blackie.

"You start at the ground next to his front leg," the judge said, looking up at me.

The judge laid his right hand on Blackie's leg, right on top of the hoof. He then placed his left hand above his right, and he kept doing this—laying one hand above the other—all the way up Blackie's leg.

"You stop at the withers," the judge said once he'd reached Blackie's mane.

I nodded when the judge said this, even though I didn't know what *withers* were. It was one of those words I'd seen in the 4-H manuals but never bothered to look up—like *snaffle* and *hippology* and *haunches*. The judge pointed to the lump where Blackie's shoulder meets his back, and I recognized it from our rides around the farm. When I first started riding Blackie, the withers were where I would rest after a long ride. I would lean forward and fold my torso over the saddle's horn, resting my forearms on Blackie's withers. They were bony and uncomfortable. I'd run my hands over that lump multiple times, curious about why it was there but never really thinking much of it. It was just another part of my pony.

"Do you know why we measure to the withers?"

Again, I stared back at the judge blankly and wondered why he kept asking me questions I didn't know the answers to.

"The withers never change," the judge said.

The judge made a few notes on his clipboard and then told me that the interview was over. He handed me a blue ribbon, which I was a little surprised by because I had failed to answer so many of his questions. My mother, who had been standing nearby, came over and helped me put Blackie back into his stall. I then lifted myself up so I was resting on the top of the stall's gate, watching Blackie. I let my cast dangle over the edge of the gate. Instead of turning around to face me, Blackie pointed his butt in my direction.

I had been looking for something unusual about my pony and found it in a very ordinary part of his body, this knob at the end of his mane that the judge said would never change. Blackie's withers made me wonder about my own body, if there was a part of me that made me more than just another same-same, Midwestern boy. As a child, I loved the stories of everyday boys and girls becoming extraordinary (or at least a little less ordinary). I sought out these stories at my hometown drugstore, where I read *X-Men* comics with a particular interest in when these characters first realized they had "powers," and at my town's public library, where I read stories of mischievous boys sneaking onto pirate ships or jumping railroad cars. I saw myself in these seemingly normal protagonists, and I cherished reading about their acts of discovery in finding themselves. It gave me comfort to know that I was just another boy in a long line of boys worried about getting lost in a sea of ordinariness and that one day I would have the chance to find my own withers, to show others what set me apart.

~

For the costume competition at that first county fair, my mother had dressed me as a hobo. She'd untucked half of my white shirt and made me wear a faded black vest, which she'd lopsidedly buttoned so I looked messy and disheveled, as if I'd slept under a bridge. She'd taped the stick of my red hobo bundle to my shoulder so it wouldn't fall off during the competition and wrapped a bandana around my neck. Then she'd teased out Blackie's mane to make him look sloppy and unkempt. The only thing missing was a tin cup with a few nickels in it—something I could shake at the crowd for a few laughs—but holding the cup while riding around the arena would have been impossible with a cast on my arm.

I don't know why she dressed me as a hobo. I already looked pathetic enough trying to ride my graying pony around the county fair arena with one good arm. She probably thought the hobo costume would elicit sympathy from the crowd and make the judge feel sorry for me. Maybe she thought I could milk some comedy out of the performance in the vein of Charlie Chaplin's Little Tramp. Or maybe she just found it funny to dress an eight-year-old boy as a hobo. If she hadn't been extra-affectionate with me after I broke my wrist, I would have thought it was some twisted plot to humiliate me.

Looking back at it now, I'm guessing my mother saw something of this hobo in my future, this outsider, this misfit, this wandering boy who didn't really belong anywhere.

"How does that feel?" my mother asked once I was atop my pony, my hobo bundle balanced on my shoulder.

"Fine," I replied, looking out over the arena where a lone girl—my only competitor—was trotting around the ring. She was dressed as a Native American chieftess. She wore a buckskin dress with jewels and sequins around the waist and collar. On her head, she had a headdress with red-tipped feathers, which cascaded off her head and down her back. She rode a handsome, leggy quarter horse, bareback. There were feathers attached to the halter in various places and buckles that shined and sparkled in the sunlight. She looked beautiful gracefully riding her horse around the arena, her body rising and falling with the motions, as if she'd galloped right out of one of the westerns my father liked to watch on TV.

I pulled the reins to the right to get Blackie walking along the edge of the arena. The reins were knotted together and looped around the saddle horn so I wouldn't drop them. All I had to do was pull the reins in one direction and Blackie would go that way. I didn't know what to do with my casted arm, so I let it hang at my side.

Across the arena, I could see my mother standing near the gate. She was talking to one of the other 4-H moms. She'd been doing this a lot during the fair, talking to other parents to get tips and information about different competitions and contests. She was competitive like that, always trying to find ways to show her creative side through her children but also looking for ways to impress others. Once, during our hometown Fourth of July parade, she dressed me as a clown, stuffed a string of tied-together scarves into one of my deep pockets, and instructed me to look surprised as I slowly pulled the scarves out and showed them to the crowd. I practiced that routine for days, trying to get the timing just right and attempting different facial expressions in the mirror. When I performed it during the parade, I let go of the wagon I was pulling—which contained my sister and my little brother Bo—and I stood in the middle of main street, looking all surprised when the string of scarves coming out of my pants went on and on and on. The crowd loved it.

As I rode Blackie around the arena, I once again felt like I needed to put on a show. I started to wave with my casted arm, but that felt wrong—*Do hobos wave?*—so I stopped. Instead, I tried to look sad holding onto the saddle's horn with my good hand as Blackie slowly walked around the arena. The women and children watched me intensely. They had these worried looks on their faces, their eyebrows furrowed a bit, their heads cocked slightly to the side, their eyes all puppy-dog-like.

They were giving me the same looks my classmates had given me when I returned to school with a broken arm—looks of both pity and wonder. Almost a month earlier, I had broken my wrist while racing against a classmate on the slick grass. The next day—the last day of school— the cafeteria was closed, so everyone had to bring a sack lunch, which we ate in our classroom after we helped our teacher clean and get the classroom ready for summer. For some reason, my mother had packed me an orange, which was difficult to peel with one arm in a cast and sling, so I handed it to Scott, the classmate I had chosen to be my "helper" that day. Earlier, after everyone had signed my cast and asked me if my arm hurt, the teacher had let me choose one of my class- mates to help me during the day, a little helper for me to boss around. Surprisingly, everyone wanted to do it. It was the only time that year when everyone wanted to be my friend. My classmates' fascination with my cast told me that everything natural and normal about me—my face, my hair, my walk, my laugh, everything—wasn't worth noticing. Only when I introduced something unnatural did my classmates start to see me.

Riding Blackie around the arena, I realized the power of being a boy with a cast. I had something no other boy or girl at the fair had, a golden ticket to get people to look at me differently, to make myself stand out. That cast was the only distinct thing about me; it set me apart from all the other boys. It took attention away from the beautiful high school girl pretending to be Native American. The crowd pitied me and my sad pony, and I liked it. Just as I had when I was the clown pulling scarves from his pocket in the parade, I looked back at the crowd and smiled.

The cast was temporary; a few months after the fair it was gone. But the lesson I took away from watching the way people reacted to my cast remained for much of that summer and into the next school year. The cast was my ticket to get people to notice me, and I couldn't help wondering what would happen when that one thing that made me special—that made me stand out, that made everyone want to be my friend—was removed from my wrist and tossed away. What would happen then? Was it crazy to want to never remove the cast—to keep my wrist wrapped up, preserved, the same forever? If I could keep the cast intact, maybe everyone would see me as more than just an ordinary boy.

~

While Blackie's withers helped me recognize my pony as special, it was his speed that really impressed me and made me wonder whether he was more than just this ordinary pony I'd imagined him to be.

After that first county fair, we tried to train Blackie in several different 4-H competitions—western horsemanship, reining, trail riding. He was horrible in all of them. He'd buck and stomp his feet and whinny these awful high-pitched neighs. He didn't have the patience to learn new tricks like reining patterns or backing through obstacles or jumping over logs. Instead, my mother decided that we would focus on Blackie's speed and that we'd train him for pole and barrel racing.

Three summers after that first county fair, we attended our first barrel racing event at an arena on the edge of town. I sat atop Blackie, wearing jeans, cowboy boots, my own bolo tie, and a western-style button-up shirt like the ones my father wore. I could feel Blackie's heat beneath me, radiating out of him. I hadn't ridden Blackie in three days because I wanted to harness all his energy and speed for this competition, bottle it all up as if that would make him go faster. My mother stood next to Blackie, holding his halter.

"Ready," my mother said, looking up at me.

I nodded, and she led us through the arena's gate. Once we entered the arena, we had a minute to get ourselves situated. My mother liked to think that Blackie could simply look at the barrels' course and know exactly what to do; all he really needed was a little winding up—as if he were a toy that would shoot off across a table after a few twists of a crank. She held Blackie's halter under his chin, letting him take in the course—the two barrels on either side of the arena and the third barrel centered, way at the other end.

I also needed to prepare myself. Running the barrels was a rush of adrenaline. It made me feel tough, invincible, free. I pushed my butt back into the saddle and grabbed tightly onto the reins. I then gave the withers a quick rub for good luck. I'd adopted that ritual after the first county fair, and whenever I was riding Blackie around the farm or before events like this, I'd rub the bony withers and send a wish out into the world. I wished for all kinds of things—for my brother to stop fighting with me, for straight As on my next report card, for the fastest time of all the participants, for chocolate ice cream for dessert. Mostly, though, I wished for people to notice me, especially after the cast was removed from my arm.

My mother looked up, and after I gave her another nod, she stepped forward, extended her arm outward, and started pulling Blackie around her body, in a circle. She did this once, twice, and then, when she felt Blackie was fully wound up, she released Blackie's halter, sending us racing onto the course.

I was dizzy from the spinning, but I held tightly onto the horn of the saddle and leaned forward slightly as we approached that first turn.

The turn around that first barrel set the tone for the entire run, so I knew I'd have to get it right. I leaned to the right, my right leg tight against Blackie's ribs, and gently yanked the reins, pulling Blackie around the first barrel clockwise. I could feel the rhythm of Blackie's movements, the up and down, the pulsing of his body releasing all that pent-up energy and turning it into speed. I kept my leg pressed against Blackie's ribs so that I wouldn't accidentally knock over the barrel as I went around it, disqualifying us.

Once we'd cleared the first barrel, I gave Blackie a tiny kick in the ribs with my heel. The second barrel was probably the easiest. We entered the second barrel's orbit at the 2 o'clock mark. I pulled the reins to the left this time, so we'd go around counterclockwise. I could hear Blackie's hooves hit the dirt and the huffing and puffing of his breath. I could see the sweat darkening his mane and the way he stared straight ahead, determined to get it all over with. For a moment, I wanted to put Blackie on autopilot, to just let him make all the moves himself because I knew he could do it, but then I remembered what my mother said when I'd mentioned this to her before. Blackie needed me there to direct him. He was old and stubborn, and if I wasn't there to pull the reins and steer him through the course, he'd veer off, do his own thing, or, even worse, just stop. I had to remember that we were a team.

When I practiced with Blackie at home—in the field next to our driveway—the final barrel was probably the trickiest of all because you wanted to go around it as tight as possible, so you'd have a straight shot to the finish line. I bent forward even more—in preparation for that final stretch—and after I'd steered Blackie around that final barrel, I gave him a couple kicks in the haunches and held onto the saddle horn as we flew like wind down the length of the arena, toward the gate and my waiting mother.

The final stretch was right down the middle of the arena—where everyone could see you—so I liked to imagine that the entire crowd went silent when they saw Blackie round that last barrel, that everyone just stared at a boy and his fast pony flying down the length of that arena, faster and faster with each step until they crossed the invisible finish line to applause and cheers.

When I was racing down that final stretch, Blackie was no longer the ratty pony my father brought to our farm one day. He was a black stallion, stealthy and quick, and I was the boy who had tamed him, who'd taught him to harness all that energy and turn it into speed. Separately, we were just an old pony and an ordinary boy. But together we were something extra, something special, something worth looking at. Within these connections with other living creatures is sometimes where the magic lives.

Blackie was never the most graceful or the most beautiful or even the fastest horse at the fairs and competitions we took him to. But that is exactly why I liked him. He came into my life when I didn't think I was special either, that nothing I did was as good as what other kids my age did. I like to think we found ourselves together, that without the other we would have been just a couple of ordinary things groping around in the dark.

~

There's a line in the Jenny Lewis song "Head Underwater" that's been stuck in my head for days. It plays on a loop in the back of my mind as

I buy groceries or drive home from work, while watching reruns or out walking my pug. It's a song about perseverance—surviving—but this one line speaks to the ordinary boy I used to be—the boy who didn't think he was anything special. The line comes about halfway into the song, delivered with a sweet sadness that makes me remember how much this boy wanted to be something unusual. It is a line about everyone having that special spark inside of them.

When I get in this melancholy mood where I fear that the boy I used to be became a very basic, very ordinary man—a mood that creeps up more and more often these days—I try to think about this line and the boy with the cast looking for the extraordinary and the pony that helped him see the magic in the everyday. I close my eyes and imagine Blackie running through tall grass, galloping away, swiftly, gracefully, no destination in mind. He isn't grumpy or stubborn. He doesn't show his teeth. There are no white patches in his hair, no graying mane. He is young, virile, buoyant. There is a fierceness to the way he moves, an intensity in his face, a determination. The pale rays of moonlight make his mane shine and sparkle. His hooves float above the grass, the blades bending and springing back up as he gently hurdles over them. Instead of the lumbering sound of hooves racing across the prairie, there is only the sound of wind.

I imagine myself with Blackie, on his back, folded over the horn of the saddle, his mane whipping up into my face as I search the passing prairie for something—I don't know what—one hand holding the reins, the other rubbing Blackie's withers, sending wish after wish out into the unknown.

Battle Buddy

Stark doesn't like anything about basic training. He complains about it all—the early-morning runs with screaming drill sergeants, the seemingly random locker searches in the middle of the night, the unforgiving Missouri heat that beats down on us on the M16 practice range. He hates the chow. He hates the low water pressure in the showers. He hates the BCGs ("Birth Control Glasses") the Army makes him wear. He complains that nobody is sending him mail, that nobody cares that he's here. When Stark's not around, we complain about *him*, how one day he'll get us all in trouble when one of the drill sergeants overhears his griping.

I'm hanging out behind the chow hall, on the loading dock, with Stark and two guys from First Platoon, eating Hostess cupcakes left over from lunch and talking about recruits who have dropped out. It's early September, a month after my eighteenth birthday, and we're five weeks into the nine-week Army basic training program at Fort Leonard Wood, Missouri. We've just finished KP duty and the woman who runs the mess hall said we could eat the cupcakes, but we had to hurry. We had to report back to the barracks soon, back to drill sergeants and training and all the camaraderie that comes with going through this hell together.

Stark sits on an empty milk crate, a chocolate cupcake in his hand. He's angry because he thinks KP duty should be reserved for the dropouts who quit during the first three weeks. Basic training is divided into three phases, and during the first phase—the Patriot Phase—a few recruits couldn't hack it and quit. We still see them in the barracks and during formations, but they don't train with us. We've heard rumors that they do odd jobs around base—painting curbs, mowing lawns, mopping hallways, KP duty. We've heard that the Army takes its time processing their paperwork, that the dropouts must wait until we graduate to go home. Stark is offended because, when he was chosen for KP duty this morning, he believes the drill sergeants mistakenly thought he was one of the dropouts.

I've been thinking about the dropouts a lot because I could easily have become one of them. I'm not your normal recruit. I'm not athletic, not into guns, not obsessed with warfare or strategic maneuvers or blowing shit up. During the Patriot Phase, I wondered why I was even in basic training. Most of the other recruits got excited about everything—disassembling and reassembling their M16s, marching around base, taking each other down during hand-to-hand combat training. None of that excited me, so I just watched the other recruits, tried to muster excitement myself, and occasionally thought about dropping out, throwing up my hands and telling the drill sergeants that I'd had enough.

Now, in the second phase of basic training—the Gunfighter Phase—I worry about failing and having to do everything over again. If you fail the marksmanship course or the hand grenade course or the PT test or any of the other checkpoints during the Gunfighter Phase, you don't get to paint curbs or wash dishes with the dropouts. You must start the phase all over with a new group of recruits.

"I'm going to graduate," Stark says, confidently, taking the last bite of his cupcake and wiping his hands on his cargo pants. "And I shouldn't be doing KP."

It is hot on this loading dock in Missouri, blazingly hot, and I keep having to wipe beads of sweat onto my sleeve. I nod along to Stark's comment. If I've learned anything during the Patriot Phase, it's that I need to trust the men around me. Back home, all my closest friends are women. But here, I'm surrounded by men—grunting, gun-loving, gung-ho men. Like me, but not. And I've had to figure out how to survive among them. I've learned to make myself invisible, to be the shadow nobody sees. I don't raise my hand when drill sergeants ask for volunteers. I don't take the lead during the tactical marches around base or during the obstacle course. I don't speak unless directly spoken to. Instead, I slink along the perimeter, watching, listening, trying to mimic what I see and hear. I stick closely to these men; I latch on, keep my head down, and follow along.

I stand up, brush the crumbs off my uniform, wipe my mouth along my cuff. As a result of my basic training strategy of being invisible, I now think the drill sergeants perceive me as one of the dropouts too—nothing special, not a leader but a follower, someone who *may* squeak by if he doesn't eventually drop out—and Stark, with his latest complaint, has got me thinking about how I can shake this image. *How do you change the way people see you when you've spent so much time manufacturing the image you want them to see?*

Just before Stark and I return to our barracks, one of the guys from first platoon asks us about "getting smoked."

I think about "getting smoked" a lot. To "smoke" someone during basic training is to punish them with physical activity. Push-ups, burpees, laps around the barracks. There are a million ways to smoke a recruit. I've heard a lot of rumors about these different ways, and I've imagined the drill sergeants sitting around thinking of *new* ways to smoke us. One afternoon someone started talking about something called The Pit, where drill sergeants smoke recruits in a Quonset hut filled with wood chips. When I first heard this, I imagined something like the pole-barn on the farm where I grew up. I imagined steel siding and sunlight pouring in from the open door, making the dust sparkle as we kicked the wood chips around. It seemed so innocent and nonthreatening—*sparkling chips of wood!*—but I knew it wasn't. I knew it was worse than the rumor made it seem.

"Have you guys been in The Sweatbox yet?" First-Platoon asks.

Stark and I shake our heads.

"Drill sergeants lock everyone inside a room, close the windows, and smoke everyone until there's a pool of sweat on the floor," First-Platoon says. "It's modeled after a torture technique."

My mind skips right over the torture part, and instead, as I walk with Stark back to the barracks, I picture a sauna, steam rising from the ground, the air heavy with moisture, barefoot men in white towels. It sounds almost peaceful.

We find the rest of the platoon cleaning their gas masks and shining their boots in our room in the barracks. There are eight beds, eight lockers, but only six men in our room because two have already dropped out. My bunk is the top one near the window, on the right side, and directly across from me is Kevlock. He's the classic all-American, boy-next-door type I've seen on afterschool specials and teen movies. He has a handsome face, a perfect smile, dimples. I noticed him the first day of basic training, and later, when we sat next to each other while riding the bus across the base, he introduced himself and I could tell we would get along.

Kevlock shares a bunk with Trumble. Trumble is small, mousy, a little nerdy. He's going into Intelligence, and, when I first met him and heard him talk, I understood why. He is matter-of-fact, likes to do everything by the book, knows a lot of random stuff about the military. He has a sort of intensity that makes it difficult for me to talk to him because I don't know what to say.

I sit down next to Gonzalez, my "battle buddy." We've been matched up, assigned to watch out for each other during basic training, because that's what the Army does; it pairs you up with someone unlike you to see how you handle difference and responsibility. They call it the "battle buddy system." I'm responsible for him, and he's responsible for me.

Every morning, after we get dressed, I'm supposed to make sure my battle buddy is "squared away," his uniform on correctly, his pockets all buttoned, his cover evenly placed atop his head, his boots shined and laced up correctly. In formation and during training, I'm supposed to keep an eye on him, make sure he is always in sight, and, whenever I can, I'm supposed to check in with him to see if he's doing all right. I'm supposed to make sure he isn't too sad, that the drill sergeants haven't beaten the spirit out of him, that he still feels good about becoming a soldier.

I'm supposed to do all these things, but I don't, and I know this makes me a bad soldier. I just don't have time. I'm too worried about failing or dropping out.

When the drill sergeants told us about the battle buddy program in week 1, I laughed to myself because I hate the word *buddy*. It sounds so juvenile. *Buddy*. Something you'd call a dog or a pony, not another soldier. I know other guys call their male friends their *buddies*, but I've never really had a close friendship with another guy, one that would justify using the word *buddy*, and I've never called my brothers *buddy*, so saying it now, at basic training, feels awkward and off.

So, I don't call Gonzalez my battle buddy, even though I'm supposed to, partially because I hate the phrase but mostly because I don't really get along with Gonzalez. We're too different, don't have anything to talk about. We're both a little shy; neither of us tries to get to know the other. Instead, I silently wish my battle buddy were someone else, someone I had more in common with. I don't say it to Gonzalez, but I've already picked out a new battle buddy.

Stark sits down next to me, leans in toward the group, and says, "Have you guys heard about The Sweatbox?"

~

I'm in formation, between Kevlock and Gonzalez, when I hear the drill sergeant bark, "Open ranks, *MARCH!*" I take one step back, trying to stay in sync with the other soldiers in my squad. The "open ranks, *MARCH*" command usually means one of two things: inspection or getting smoked.

It's a few days after KP duty with Stark, and we're practicing doing things together as a platoon. In the Gunfighter Phase, we're supposed to function as a unit, in sync. This is the phase where we get to fire our rifles and throw grenades and complete an obstacle course, but it is also when we are expected to gel with the men and women in our platoon. If we don't work together or if we fail the GO/NO GO tests at the end of the Gunfighter Phase, we can't move on to phase 3—the Warrior Phase—where all the cool stuff takes place, like bivouac and field training exercises.

"Half right, *FACE!*" the drill sergeant barks.

I almost let out a groan because I know what's coming next.

During the Patriot Phase, the drill sergeants smoked us for every minor infraction. We got smoked for holding our fake rifles upside down. We got smoked for falling out of step while marching. We got

smoked when the pockets on our cargo pants weren't properly buttoned. We quickly learned to get things right the first time, to pay
attention to details, to listen and observe.

Now, in the Gunfighter Phase, they seem to smoke us for no appar-
ent reason, just because they can.

"Front-Leaning Rest Position, *MOVE!*" the drill sergeant yells, and I
hop down into the starting position for a push-up, arms fully extended,
back and legs straight like a plank.

I don't know why the drill sergeants insist on calling this the "Front-
Leaning Rest Position." It's not really a *resting* position. It's a position of
discomfort. It makes our backs ache and our arms wobble, especially
when the drill sergeants make us hold it for long periods of time. It is
supposed to strengthen our arms and tighten our abs, but during the
first few weeks of basic training, we'd squirm and sigh and shift around
to relieve the pain. The drill sergeants, of course, loved to see us squirm.
They liked it when our arms would wobble and shake or when our
backs would begin to get sore and we'd raise our butts to take off the
pressure. They especially liked to see us give up completely, when we'd
drop our chests to the ground and let out a sigh of relief, because then
they had reason to smoke us.

Just when my arms begin to wobble, the drill sergeant yells, "DOWN,"
and I lower my body to the ground. A second later, the drill sergeant
yells, "UP," and I slowly push myself back into the plank position.

The push-up part isn't that hard; my back is getting a little sore, but
my arms are strong enough to do a few push-ups. What's difficult is staying in sync with everyone else. I'm supposed to keep my battle buddy
in the corner of my eye, and when the drill sergeant yells DOWN, I'm
supposed to lower myself in sync with my battle buddy. If I don't stay
in sync with him, the drill sergeant will come running over and smoke
us both. Now that we're in the Gunfighter Phase, when you make a mistake, you and your battle buddy get smoked together because you're
responsible for each other; it's *your* fault he isn't in sync with you.

The drill sergeant is calling out cadence—*DOWN, UP, DOWN, UP*—
and I can already tell that I'm not in sync with Gonzalez, so I try something else. Instead of watching Gonzalez to my left, I shift my gaze

over to the other side, so I can see Kevlock. As I'm doing the push-ups, I keep an eye on Kevlock, watching the way he stares straight at the ground as he lowers himself, the way his shoulders hover over his hands, the way his forearms and triceps tighten and flex as he pushes himself back up. I try not to get too wrapped up in watching Kevlock, but I can't help myself. He seems so confident and controlled, and after watching him for a few minutes, I am back in sync.

Now, when he goes down, I go down, and when he comes back up, I come back up, too.

~

We're on our way to marksmanship training at the rifle range and Kevlock and I are sitting together on the bus.

It doesn't always work out this way. When the drill sergeant yells, "FALL OUT," we're supposed to quickly fall into line near the door of the bus, paying little regard to who is standing in front or behind us. But I always make a point of standing next to Kevlock in formation, and when the drill sergeant releases us, I keep my eye on Kevlock and position myself behind him in line. This way, when we get onto the bus, I have a better chance of sharing a seat with him.

The bus rides across base have become my favorite part of basic training. They are a reprieve, a time to center myself and catch my breath. They remind me of being a kid, when I'd ride the bus into town for school. I learned a lot about people from those bus rides. I learned to listen. I learned what to share and what not to share. I learned to tolerate my surroundings. I learned to tune out what I didn't like and to focus on what I did.

In our seat near the back of the bus, I watch Kevlock reach down and unbutton the cargo pocket on his right thigh. All recruits are required to keep the *Soldier's Manual of Common Tasks* in their right thigh cargo pocket. During our first week, the drill sergeants told us to take out the *Soldier's Manual* any time we had downtime, when we weren't training or running or listening to them speak. *It is good to know the basic skills*, they said. *There will be a test.* Most of us don't take their advice. Most of us take out the *Soldier's Manual* on the bus and pretend to read from it while talking quietly to the soldier next to us. Only Trumble and maybe a few others actually read their manuals during downtime.

I take out my *Soldier's Manual* and begin flipping through the pages. The tasks in the manual are divided into sections based on the six common tasks for skill level 1: *SEE, COMMUNICATE, NAVIGATE, SHOOT, SURVIVE,* and *HANDLE REMAINS.* I pause at the beginning of the SHOOT section.

Kevlock leans in a little bit and looks over at me.

"Are you nervous about qualifying with the M16?" he asks.

I am. He knows I am, so I nod.

"The drill sergeants made me practice shooting with my left hand, even though I'm right-handed," I say, "since my left eye is my dominant eye."

Last week, we went to practice our marksmanship and Drill Sergeant Warren knelt next to me and told me to switch arms. He wasn't yelling or screaming, and for once it almost seemed tender, like he was my father or uncle or an older brother I never had.

"Do you fire rifles back home?" Kevlock asks.

I tell him about the time I went deer hunting with my father and brother. While they went to flush out a deer from the brush, I stood near the truck shivering, barely holding the rifle in my cold hands. I didn't really want to be there; I had no interest in hunting. I did it because my father needed a third person and I didn't want to disappoint him.

"Do you think it's weird for a guy who doesn't like guns to enlist in the army?" I ask.

He shakes his head.

"Not at all," he says. "It takes all types."

Kevlock smiles and then looks down at the *Soldier's Manual* in his hands. I look out the bus window. The bus is just pulling up to the rifle range. I look back at Kevlock. I want to be completely invisible during basic training, but I know I can't do that. I need *someone,* a real battle buddy, the one person who sees me for who I really am, and I think I've found that someone in Kevlock. I feel like there is this force field around him, and all I need to do is let myself be pulled in.

$\sim$

The drill sergeant hands me the grenade. It's a fake, like the M16s we practiced with at the beginning of basic training. The grenade is heavier than it should be. I turn it around in my hand, trying to look inside, to see if there is something there that shouldn't be. I notice a small hole at the bottom, and when I turn the grenade so I can look at the hole more closely, white marshmallow cream starts gushing out. I lob the grenade out into the field. It flies out a little ways, but then turns and comes flying back at me, like a boomerang. I duck and the grenade explodes behind me. The drill sergeant doesn't flinch. He marks my helmet with an X, to indicate that I failed, then hands me a second grenade. Same thing happens. *Marshmallow, lob, boomerang, explosion, X.* He hands me a third grenade, a fourth, a fifth, each time with the same result. *Marshmallow, lob, boomerang, explosion, X. Marshmallow, lob, boomerang, explosion, X.*

I open my eyes, shake away the dream, and hear a low yelp, like someone standing at the end of a long tunnel yelling. It repeats, gets a little louder. Then it comes again, this time almost audible. I realize that one of the drill sergeants is yelling as he walks down the hallway.

"Get *UUUUUP!* Get *UUUUUP!*" the drill sergeant bellows. "Get *UUUUUUP!*"

It is the middle of the night and we're about to get smoked. I bolt upright, jump down from the top bunk, and stand at the end of my bed, barefoot, my T-shirt half untucked.

This has happened before. Sometimes the drill sergeants just yell. They make us stand at attention at the end of our bunks while they go from room to room yelling, sometimes getting in our faces. Other times we're ordered to do push-ups, which are difficult when you're still half asleep. Once, they summoned us all to the briefing room at the end of the hall and smoked us all together by keeping us in the Front-Leaning Rest Position until they felt we had been punished enough.

I'm exhausted, barely able to keep my eyes open. The Gunfighter Phase has turned me into a deep sleeper. The long days practicing marksmanship on the rifle range. The obstacle course with the tall wooden walls and barbed wire we had to low-crawl under. The land navigation trainings in the sweltering Quonset huts, where the drill sergeants would

take us to the back of the room and smoke us if we fell asleep. Being
constantly on alert, aware enough to know when you're about to make
a mistake.

Kevlock stands directly across from me. We're both standing in the
position of attention—backs stiff, arms at our sides, heads up, half-
open eyes trying to look straight ahead. I try not to stare at Kevlock.
Instead, I look at a point above his head, at the whiteness of the wall,
and occasionally, when the drill sergeant isn't near, I sneak glances at
him and try to stop myself from smiling.

I stare at Kevlock because I like looking at him, but also because
every time I do I feel something more than just attraction. The feeling
seems more intense, more real, something I can't quite put my finger
on. It could be that all the forced proximity of basic training, living
and running and marching and doing everything with the same group
of men, has created this feeling. All this togetherness has created a
bond of brotherhood, and because I don't really know what that bond
should feel like, I imagine that it feels like this, like electric current pul-
sating through your veins. I've felt tinges of attraction toward guys
before, but never like this. Never this intense. Never this real.

Kevlock is right there, across from me, every morning and every
night, and inside I feel this pulsing every time I see him. I don't know
what to do with all this bottled-up energy, so I just stare.

The drill sergeant pops his head inside our room and yells *"FRONT-
LEANING REST POSITION, MOVE!"*

I sigh and hop down into position.

∼

Here are the conditions: Your battle buddy is bleeding. The blood is
coming from a wound in his forearm, just below the elbow. You've
applied a field and pressure dressing to the wound but the blood keeps
coming. It is bright red, and it is gushing down your battle buddy's arm.
Thankfully, your battle buddy is still breathing. You tell him that the
field dressing did not stop the bright red bleeding. You find a couple
sticks nearby and from your T-shirt you rip off a few strips of brown

cloth. You need to apply a tourniquet to stop the bright red bleeding. The tourniquet stick shouldn't unwind.

I'm sitting with Kevlock, Gonzalez, and Trumble, on the grass in the shade outside our barracks, waiting for Donovan—our platoon leader—to hand out supplies so we can start practicing applying tourniquets. It's hot, and we're in our brown T-shirts. The drill sergeants aren't around.

Donovan drops off a couple sticks and strips of cloth and tells us to apply a tourniquet to our battle buddies but not to twist the stick. *Simulate the rest*, he says.

I grab a stick and a strip of cloth and turn to Kevlock.

"Roll up your sleeve," I say to him.

Before Kevlock can roll up his sleeve, we're interrupted.

"You're supposed to do this with *your* battle buddy," Trumble says to me.

At first I think he's joking, that it doesn't really matter who we practice on. But then I remember what kind of guy Trumble is. He does everything by the book, and when the instructions are to practice on our battle buddies, he will make sure the instructions are followed.

Trumble is looking right at me, and out of the corner of my eye I can see that Gonzalez is, too. Trumble's eyes are dark, his brow furrowed a little. He's scowling.

I let out a nervous laugh. In my gut, I feel the deep sting of Trumble's words, and I wonder if he knows that my fascination with Kevlock is more than just friendship. He's been watching me spend all this time with his battle buddy, during bus rides and while we're sitting around during our down time. He must know that something is up.

I look at Kevlock. He doesn't look me in the eye. Instead, he stares at his boots. *His* look—one that seems to signify agreement with Trumble by saying nothing—stings even deeper.

I want to forget what Trumble said and the way Kevlock wouldn't look at me, but I can't. While I practice applying a tourniquet to Gonzalez's arm and while I'm reading the steps in the *Soldier's Manual of Common Tasks* to make sure I'm doing it right, I think about what I did wrong. I didn't know there were rules about the way battle buddies should act in basic training, that there was this imaginary line between support and something else (neediness? desire?) that battle buddies weren't supposed to cross. I just wanted to fit in, to belong, and I thought latching onto Kevlock was the way to do that.

Gonzalez starts applying a tourniquet to my arm. He ties a strip of cloth around my bicep, a few inches above the imaginary wound on my forearm. He has the *Soldier's Manual of Common Tasks* open and is following the steps. He ties a half knot and places a stick over the knot. I close my eyes. In my head, I imagine bright red blood dripping onto the grass. I picture Gonzalez finishing a full knot, and instead of stopping there, he starts twisting the stick clockwise. He winds the stick a few turns and then lets Trumble take over. Trumble winds the tourniquet with both hands, slowly at first. The bandage tightens around my bicep and I can hear my blood pumping in my ears. The bright red bleeding has stopped. Then, Trumble lets go of the stick. The stick unwinds and the bleeding starts again, this time spouting out in big, bright spurts. Trumble grabs hold of the stick and starts twisting again, faster this time, more intense, turning and winding until my arm separates from the rest of my body and falls onto the grass.

Then there is only the pulsing and throbbing of one limb separated, disconnected from everything else.

$\sim$

The drill sergeants' favorite way to smoke us is to make us run around the water tower. If we don't fall into formation correctly or don't stay in Front-Leaning Rest Position or sigh too loudly, they'll yell, *"HIT THE TOWER!"* and point at the blue water tower in the grassy square outside our barracks.

We're halfway to the water tower now, laughing at Drill Sergeant Groth, the only black, female drill sergeant in our company, because there is something unintentionally funny about the way she tells us to *"HIT THE TOWER!"*

It is Saturday, and we are groggy from the long week of marksmanship and hand grenade training. Drill Sergeant Groth noticed this right after we fell into formation. She started by making us do push-ups, but when we were too slow, she barked, "Oh, so youuuu don't wanna move? *HIT THE TOWER!*" and pointed off in the direction of the tower. The word *hit* came off sharp and shrill, and we ran off toward the tower giggling.

During the Patriot Phase, when we were learning to simply follow directions, the drill sergeants would make us hit the water tower alone. They would yell our name and point, and we'd have to peel ourselves away from the platoon and dash off toward the tower. Getting smoked this way was the worst. It felt solitary and lonely during a time when I didn't want to feel alone. It reminded me of summer camp as a kid, when I got called out for having my elbows on the table during lunch and the entire camp chanted while I, embarrassed, stared at my hands: *Bronson, Bronson, strong and able / get your elbows off the table. / This is not a horse's stable. / But a decent dining table. / 'Round the mess hall you must go. / You must go. / You must go.*

I'm near the back of the pack as we make our way around the tower, further behind than I want to be but still keeping up. I can feel my dog tags smacking against my chest. I reach out and slap the steel legs of the tower as we pass, like everyone else. On the way back from the tower, I look around. Gonzalez is beside me like a good battle buddy. Stark and Donovan are just behind me. I don't see Trumble at all. Then I spot Kevlock just ahead of me, and I remember how he looked away when Trumble said, *You're supposed to do this with your battle buddy*, and how embarrassed I felt for being accused of stealing someone else's battle buddy. I've been trying to shake that scene for a few days, trying to act like everything is normal, but my memory won't let me. It keeps reminding me of all these things I don't want to remember—how Trumble scowled, how I laughed because I didn't know what else to do, how Kevlock wouldn't look at me.

In an alternative version of the tourniquet memory, I imagine Trumble not there, not able to stop me from claiming his battle buddy. I apply the tourniquet to Kevlock, holding his bicep as I wrap the cloth tightly around his arm. I put the stick in place and tie a full knot. Then, I look up at him and ask, *How's that? Too tight?* When he says *no*, I twist the tourniquet just a tiny bit, testing to see how far he will let me go.

∼

I'm in formation, between Kevlock and Gonzalez, when Drill Sergeant Warren tells us that today will be a "free day" away from base. We're told that the free day is sponsored by a church, that there will be pizza and bowling, and that we will be able to buy whatever other snacks we want, that there will be time to relax and not think about M16s and military maneuvers and whether we'll pass our physical fitness test— which is coming up in a week. We're told that the drill sergeants won't be there, but we must be on our best behavior because we represent the base. We're also told that the free day isn't mandatory, but if we opt not to go, we must stay on base and clean.

Drill Sergeant Warren tells us we have fifteen minutes to change into our civilian clothes and meet the buses next to the barracks. As I climb the barrack stairs to my locker, I think about how awkward wearing civilian clothes will feel. I've gotten so used to cinching up this belt and making sure the flaps on my cargo pants are buttoned and squaring my cover properly on my head, that for a moment, while I'm chang-ing into the jeans and shirt I wore on the flight down to Fort Leonard Wood, I worry that everything about my civilian clothes will feel wrong. Maybe that's how I'm supposed to feel.

As I'm leaving the barracks, I notice Kevlock in his civilian clothes, now a different man, and I can't help but stare. He looks so different, more relaxed. I've been lying low since Trumble called me out, avoid-ing Kevlock and Trumble as much as I possibly can.

The bus leaves the base and follows a highway littered with signs for strip clubs and gun stores and fast-food restaurants, the usual signifiers of rural America. I sit next to the window and watch everything glide by, like an inmate released into the world after years behind bars. It all seems to sparkle and shine. When we arrive at the church, the bus driver tells us the schedule and where to find everything. He points to the bowling alley and the convenience store down the street, where we can hang out and buy whatever we want. There is also a gymna-sium attached to the church, where we can play basketball and where dinner will be served. He ends by telling us what's off-limits, how we should really stick to the area between the church and the bowling alley because he doesn't want anyone running off. *You can have fun*, he says. *Just make sure you attend the church service.*

Gonzalez, Donovan, and I spend a few hours playing pool and eating junk food at the convenience store down the street. Around late afternoon, we shamble down to the gymnasium. After dinner, we are ushered into a large church chapel, where recruits fill dozens of pews. A pastor stands at the front of the chapel. Once everyone is settled, he launches into a fire-and-brimstone style sermon.

The pastor describes a girl in a car accident, how the car caught on fire and people could see her burning and hear her screaming for help, but no one did anything. *The girl was asking to be saved, but it was too late*, the pastor says. *She hadn't accepted Jesus Christ as her personal savior and would now burn for eternity.*

The pastor then calls recruits forward, tells them that if they want to be saved counselors will be on hand. I watch as several counselors appear around the edges of the church. I watch as recruits come up to the front of the chapel and bow down. I watch Donovan hug one of the counselors, tears in his eyes. He's weeping and blabbering a bit, and I can't take my eyes off him. Eventually, I turn away. I look across the church pews, and I see Kevlock.

I should be thinking about what a horrible Christian I've pretended to be, how I haven't attended church in years, how I've lied to others, to myself. But I'm not thinking any of these thoughts. I'm thinking about Kevlock, how I haven't seen him all day, how good he looks in his civilian clothes, how I just want to get back to basic training so I can be near him again.

The drill sergeants will call us into the briefing room late in the afternoon and smoke us until there is a pool of our sweat collected at our feet. There will be sweat everywhere, dripping from my forehead, coming off my clothes, being flicked up every time someone kicks their feet back and assumes the Front-Leaning Rest Position. I'll feel the moisture under my hands, against my shins when I rest them on the floor, under my sneakers as they squeak against the tiles. I'll keep up with the other soldiers, follow the drill sergeants as they call out cadence from the doorway, and I'll stare intently at Kevlock from across the room, unable to take my eyes off him. I'll think about how intense my feelings for him are and I'll speculate on what will happen once we graduate and go home. I'll wonder if these kinds of feelings even exist outside basic training or if they were simply manufactured by our circumstances—men forced to become buddies in order to get by. I'll want Kevlock to stay vibrant and beautiful in my mind forever— doing perfect push-ups, flipping through the *Soldier's Manual*, smiling like everything will work out—but I'll know that he won't, so I'll flick up sweat from the pool on the floor, stare at him, and wonder what could have been.

When I get back to the barracks, Kevlock is there, but I try not to look at him. I change out of my civilian clothes, and, without saying anything to anyone, I climb into my bunk and try to fall asleep, hoping not to dream about marshmallow grenades or failing out of basic training or The Sweatbox.

The first thing the drill sergeants do the next morning is smoke us.

Wolf Pack

We had it all figured out. We'd walk up and down the street outside Camp Casey in South Korea, and once we found a bar worth checking out, we'd go inside and see if the rumors about the juicy girls were true. We'd heard that there are girls in the bars, girls from Russia and the Philippines mostly. They'd been trained to draw soldiers in, get them to spend money, help them to have a good time. We'd heard that they dressed sexy—in shorts and low-cut tops—and that they came right up to you, sat down next to you, and talked to you in English if you agreed to buy them a drink. The soldiers on the base called the women "juicy girls." Some soldiers fell in love with the girls, we'd heard. Some spent all their money buying little glasses of juice for them.

"They call it soju," Lake says as we walk down the street. "Korean distilled alcohol. They mix it with juice."

All of this is news to me. I am tromping along behind Lake, looking at the shops and bars along the street, their garish neon signs and strange-sounding names advertising mink blankets and tailored suits and beer and dancing. There are seven of us in our little pack, all men from a National Guard platoon I've been a part of for less than a year. I hardly know most of the men, but I've learned to listen and pick up things about them. Johnson and Axemaker are both married; I know because I've heard them talk about their wives. Usually, when they mention their wives, I just nod along, unable to really say anything back. Yanni isn't married, but he's old enough to be. He has a bushy mustache like my father and these tiny glasses perched on his nose. I know almost nothing about Heilman. Lake is loud and boisterous, and for

45

these reasons most people like him. Weggy is the guy I know the best. He's younger than all the rest, probably in his early twenties, and seems the most laid back, the easiest to talk to.

I am the new guy to the platoon, only eighteen, and this is my first "summer camp"—the two weeks we train someplace away from our usual armory in North Dakota. When I heard that we were going to South Korea, I got excited because I hadn't ever left the country and everything about two weeks in a foreign place seemed exotic. On the flight over, I thought about everything I wanted to see, how I wanted to take in as much as I could, experience what it was like to be foreign in an unfamiliar place. But, because I was new, I didn't know how to act when we got to South Korea. I didn't know what to do while training and while standing around during the breaks. I was disoriented by all the novelty. So, I just did what everyone else did. When Lake asked our entire room whether we wanted to check out the village outside the gate, I nodded like everyone else and drifted along after them when they walked out the gate in search of juicy girls.

Outside Camp Casey, we wander around for a bit, gawking at how weird South Korea is. Lake has heard that the *good* juicy bars are down alleyways, so after we take a moment to orient ourselves, he steers us into the darkness of one of the alleys off the main drag.

Before Camp Casey, we spent a week at a remote outpost in northern South Korea, near the DMZ (which I saw from a fogged-up van window as we drove past). Mostly, we poured concrete and built cinderblock walls. In the evenings, there was nothing to do but play cards and make fun of one another. The men liked to tease, I learned. They teased Weggy because of his haircut. They teased one of the sergeants for bringing a loofah to summer camp. They teased me for always having my nose in a book. I never knew what to say back to these teasings. Usually, when I heard them teasing me, I looked up from my book, laughed along with them for a bit and then went back to what I was reading. But, once they turned their attention away from me, I lifted my eyes from my book and watched them. In high school, my primary friend group was made up of exclusively women, so, after basic training, I spent much of my first year in the military just watching the men around me. They all seemed so comfortable around each other, so natural in the way they teased and goofed around. I watched them and wondered why I didn't feel the same way, why I had such a hard time feeling that I belonged among them.

After second-guessing and hemming and hawing over whether to enter several different bars, we finally settle on an inconspicuous bar down one of the many shaded alleyways. As we walk into the bar, Lake tells us to be cool, to not blow it for everyone. When he says this, he looks right at me.

~

During summer camp, I felt special when I could get Lake's attention. He always seemed so confident, so sure of himself, and I admired his ability to command an audience and get everyone to go along with what he wanted. When he spoke, people listened. It was a quality that I wished I had, one I admired in athletes while watching sports in high school.

I've always had an odd relationship with team sports. In junior high, I favored individual sports like track and field because I didn't have to trust in other people. I knew my own abilities and could rely on them to achieve what I wanted. I didn't need anyone else. In high school, however, I gave up sports altogether because I wasn't very good at throwing or running or jumping. Still, I attended all the football games, mostly to watch the guys on the team. The way they stood so close to each other. The way they slapped each other on various parts of their bodies. The way they huddled together, linking arms and stomping and shouting. All of it fascinated me, mostly because there was something there I was missing out on, some kind of energy and power created by all those bodies working together as a team. I wanted to feel that.

After basic training—where I just wanted someone to help me get through the rigor of learning to be a soldier—I went looking for that collective energy. I used my powers of observation—something I'd always prided myself on—to watch the men and mimic their behaviors. I watched the way they carried themselves, the way they talked to each other, the way they joked around. Then, I tried placing myself in the middle of all that action. When we got to choose our cots in the tent at the outpost in South Korea, I chose the one in the middle, believing it would be the best place for me to blend in and observe. It was almost as if I believed I'd absorb all the masculine energy surrounding me, that some of it would rub off on me. Eventually, if I paid attention, I'd start to understand what it felt like to be a part of the pack.

∼

I try not to let Lake's remark about being cool bother me as I step inside the bar and look around. Along one wall is a long wooden bar with five or six stools along it and three tables with mismatched chairs off to the side. At the back of the room is a small dance floor and along the back wall is a door. There is music softly playing—something I don't recognize. We're the only soldiers in the place.

The bartender sees us and waves us in. We order beer, exchanging Korean won for lukewarm bottles, and then mill around the bar for a bit, unsure of what to do with ourselves. Eventually, we spread out. Axemaker, Johnson, and Newman sit at one of the low tables. Yanni settles into a stool at the end of the bar. I hang back for a little bit, but eventually I settle into a stool in the middle of the bar where everyone can see me.

Under different circumstances, I would find the small bar cozy, but there is something off about it. There's a stillness I can't explain, not dangerous or spooky, just slightly off. Something is missing, I think, remembering what Lake said about the juicy girls. I shift around nervously on the stool, looking around at the bottles behind the bar, at the speaker near the dance floor, at the door in the back of the room.

It could be that everything seems off because so much is unfamiliar to me. I'm nervous about all the firsts—my first time drinking in a bar, my first time in a foreign country, my first time out with men from my platoon during summer camp. These are the firsts that the men around me already know. They don't know that there is a whole list of other things I'm nervous about, like the possibility of a juicy girl sitting down next to me and touching my knee or my arm or any other part of me, making it my first time being touched like that by a woman. Whereas

I imagine the other men would be excited by a woman touching them in this way, the very thought of being touched like that sends a cold chill down my spine.

I try not to think about that. I try to push that thought out of my head because I don't know what I'd do if that happened.

Then the girls show up. They come through the doorway in the back of the room. Three. I don't get a good look at them at first because once I see them, I look away. I look around the room, trying to find *something* to occupy my mind—a jukebox or an interesting matchbook—but I don't know what to look at, so I just stare at my hands. Not at the door in the back of the room. Not at the girls moving across the room. Not at the guys from my platoon, watching the girls approach, whispering to each other, smiling, laughing. No. I just stare at my hands.

When I look up, one of the girls is talking to Yanni, a few stools away from me. The girl is asking if he'd like to buy her a "drinky." The other two girls are still in the back of the room. One is messing with the music. One is looking at her fingernails.

For a moment, I think about getting up and walking out the door, but I can't. We're not supposed to wander around off-base by ourselves. We're always supposed to have our "battle buddy," someone to help keep us in check. I don't have one battle buddy; I have six, and none of them look like they want to leave, so I'm stuck here.

Then I remember the newspaper. As we walked out the front gate of Camp Casey, I grabbed a local newspaper, turned it over a few times, and then stuffed it into my back pocket. I can feel it there now, sitting at the bar, so I grab it from my pocket. I unfold the paper in front of me and start to read, thinking that reading will distract my nervousness and take my mind off the juicy girls. Almost instantly, the bar seems to fade away as I read about a fundraiser by the officers' wives and sales at the PX and sporting events on base. Reading always carries me away to somewhere else.

Out of the corner of my eye, I can see the juicy girl talking to Yanni. The girl keeps touching Yanni on the elbow. One of the other girls is standing near Newman and Johnson and Axemaker, asking if they'd like to buy her a drink. The third girl is just sitting down next to Weggy. I can see it all from my stool in the middle of the bar, girls smiling and laughing and asking for drinks all around me.

I turn the page of the newspaper, read something about a training exercise south of the base, when I feel the hairs rise on the back of my neck. Someone says my name, and when I look up from the paper, everyone is staring at me.

I can feel their gaze on me.

"A newspaper? Really?" one of the older guys says from a nearby table.

He says this like I should have known better. I should have known what to do, where to look, how to act in a juicy bar. I should have known how to play it cool, seem aloof and laid back like the other men in my platoon. I should have known that you don't read a newspaper when there are pretty girls around.

I, of course, don't know any of this. I thought the men would just ignore me. But I got called out for being different, and, rather than feeling good about my uniqueness and the person I was becoming, I felt worse because it made me question my own abilities to adapt. All my military training had conditioned me to want to adapt, to blend in, and for a while I believed that that was what I wanted. To be like everyone else. Years later, I would wonder how my life would have been different if the military hadn't forced me to tamp down what made me different, if I had embraced it earlier—like many of the gay men and women I met in college—instead of running from it.

I fold the newspaper, place it on the bar, and try to act normal. I don't say anything. I hold the beer I've hardly touched in both my hands. The men seem to accept this behavior—they are satisfied with this act—so they go back to their drinks and juicy girls and stop staring at the awkward guy in the middle of the bar.

The men have a few more drinks. Weggy and Lake and Yanni all make small talk with the girls. Eventually everyone gets bored, and we decide to leave the bar and head back to base. We wander the streets a bit. The men are happy. I dawdle along behind them. Lake wants to go to one of the dance clubs, but everyone else is ready to head back to base. We find our way to the gate, and, once on base, we board the bus that loops around the perimeter. I sit near the front, alone, three rows behind the driver. The rest of the platoon sits behind me, in the back of the bus. They are laughing and talking about the night. They are giving Yanni and Weggy a hard time for the way they acted around the juicy girls. They are too preoccupied with debriefing how the night went to notice anything else around them.

I watch the men for a little bit but then look down at my hands again. I've been wringing and cracking them all night. They look rough, red. When I look up, I see a guy looking at me. He's young, maybe a year or two older than me. He sits in the second row, across the aisle from me, and when I notice him looking, he turns away. I look out the window at base as we wind our way along the perimeter, and when I look back at him, he is staring at me again. He smiles at me, and I smile back.

When we reach our stop, I exit the bus without looking at him, but once I'm standing outside, I turn and look back to see if he is watching me. He is staring at me through the glass, and I catch his eye again, recognizing something of myself in him, something I've been hiding because I didn't know there are other people who feel this way too, especially on a military base in South Korea. He stares out the window, big eyes, slight smile, something lonely yet hopeful in the way he watches me as the bus drives away, and I just stare back, not knowing what I should do, which urge I should follow—the one telling me to follow the men back to the barracks or the one telling me to chase after the bus.

How to Reintegrate

1. Tell your friends and relatives how you'd like to celebrate.

A week before flying home to North Dakota from Kosovo, tell your mother what you'd like when you return. Tell her that you'd like a nice meal, someplace casual and not too fancy, and dessert, a decadent cake or crème brûlée, stuff you can't get in the chow halls. Tell her you'd like to see her and your father but that in the evening you'd like to spend time with your friends, reconnecting after being away for seven months. Tell her that you're ready to come home. To get back to your old life. Even though you recognize that something has changed. You feel like someone else, someone different from the man who left on the peacekeeping mission. You feel like someone waiting to be born anew.

On the bus from the airport to the armory, where all the friends and family are waiting, shift nervously in your seat. Fiddle with the sleeve of your Battle Dress Uniform, which you've rolled up over your new biceps because it is August in North Dakota. *Here,* Fly says as he reaches over and smooths out the rolled fabric. As he does this, close your eyes. Feel his fingers graze your arm and remember what it felt like lifting weights with him in the makeshift gym at Camp Bondsteel in Kosovo, how he made you recognize your own desires when you watched him and felt something inside you stir. He helped you change into something new. If anyone gets credit for making this new you, it is he.

When you open your eyes, smile back at him as he pats you on your shoulder, then quickly look away. Don't reveal too much.

When the crowd of friends and family comes into view and you see your mother holding a sign that reads HAPPY BIRTHDAY BRONSON, don't say anything. It's your twentieth birthday, but you don't want to make a big deal of it. Sink down in your seat a little bit and hope no one else notices the sign. The other men and women on the bus—the ones you have spent the entire deployment with—will notice. They will slap you on the back and wish you a happy birthday and laugh when you give them your best embarrassed smile.

Hug your mother. Shake your father's hand. Answer questions about the flight, the deployment, the feeling of being home. Squint into the sun as you look around at everyone else standing in little clumps surrounded by loved ones. Fathers holding children. Husbands kissing wives. Mothers hanging off their sons. Look for Fly in the crowd but give up after a few minutes. You'll see him again at the next drill in a couple months.

When your parents ask if you are hungry, nod because you are. Then follow your parents back to their car and watch from the passenger's side as the long line of vehicles leaves the parking lot and makes its way back out into the world.

2. Try not to overbook yourself.

After your welcome-back dinner, drop your parents off at their hotel, then take their car and pick up your best friend, Beka. She is the only person you want to see.

When Beka climbs into the passenger's seat, ask her where she wants to go. When she shrugs, just drive.

Ask Beka about the summer. Ask her about the town. Ask her about everything you've missed. Notice the silence when you stop talking. Look at her and see this strange expression on her face. Ask her what is wrong. Notice the tears. Ask her again: What's wrong? Listen when she tells you that she is in love with you.

Swallow.

Blink.

Grip the steering wheel a little tighter.

Pull into a Burger King.

Look at the tan and blue and red restaurant sign. Look at the parking lot. Look up at the fading sunlight. Finally, look over at her.

Breathe.

Breathe.

Then tell her the thing you've been holding in, the thing you realized while watching Fly lift weights in Kosovo.

Tell her that you are gay.

You will be inclined to look away after saying this, to let your mind wander off and think about anything else. Try to resist this inclination. Try to look at Beka. Just for a few seconds. Resist the urge to fling open the car door and run away.

3. Allow yourself to feel all kinds of feelings.

The next week, tell more friends. Tell Niki while watching a movie at her apartment. Tell Ann when she gets off work. With each reveal, feel the weightlessness of saying what you kept hidden for so long. Take a few deep breaths and cherish not having that secret down in the pit of your stomach anymore. Then, feel the regret of not doing it sooner and the creeping dread of having to tell your parents and siblings next.

During your sophomore year of college, go to your first queer student group meeting. Introduce yourself. Smile awkwardly at everyone around you. Watch them for a bit and feel what it's like to be seen and recognized and heard. Feel tense and anxious, but also so fucking good. Light as air.

Go to the beginning-of-the-school-year picnic. Flirt. Or try to. When you notice a guy staring at you, stare back at him. Recognize that feeling again, the one you'd felt watching Fly lift weights in Kosovo. Feel it rumble around in your chest. Feel it sending electrical charges through your body. Remember those sensations when you call the guy and invite him out on a date.

Go to monthly drill and act like nothing has changed. Wear that uniform. Roll up the sleeves to show off your biceps. Polish your boots. Clean your rifle. During briefings, look at Fly and remember this man you used to be, a man just figuring out what he wanted, a man still holding so much in.

Stand in formation.

4. Talk about how you're feeling.

Go out with the man from the picnic. Get lost looking for a corn maze. Find a restaurant instead. Talk about your favorite movies and your siblings. Laugh when he knocks over his water glass. Smile when you notice that he is just as nervous as you.

When he invites you back to his dorm room, accept his invitation.

In his room, ask him about his posters. Ask him about his photographs. Ask him about his job as an RA. Tell him about your family. Your hometown. Don't mention the military or Fly or how you feel as if you're being torn in two directions.

When you both stop talking, lean forward and kiss him.

5. Be patient.

Let the years pass. Toggle between your new life out of the closet and the one where you put on camo and pretend you are someone else. Date other men. Break up with boyfriends. Once a month and two weeks in summer, return to your place in Second Squad, Second Platoon. Move on from Fly. Develop crushes on other guys in the military. Fantasize, but never act on them. You know where to draw the line.

Recognize when aspects of one world cross into the other. When you see a woman from your unit at the only gay bar in town, don't hide because you fear she'll out you to everyone in your platoon. Instead, sit down next to her and strike up a conversation. She is in a different platoon, but you recognize her from weekend drills and assume she recognizes you. Once you've had a few beers, ask her whether she knows who you are. Smile when she says "no."

Two and a half years after returning from Kosovo, one semester away from graduating college, don't answer your phone when your squad leader calls. Let it go to voicemail. Try to resist cursing loudly when you hear the message that your unit has been deployed to Iraq.

6. Focus on the positive.

There isn't much, but in Iraq, think about all the little ways you've found joy. Watching the sun rise over the reeds and radiate across the hazy sky. Throwing candy to children along the roads. Savoring the rose-flavored popsicles you find in the chow hall coolers. Chatting with a university student—your Iraqi counterpart—about Walt Whitman and Flannery O'Connor while on a mission in Baghdad. Buying *Will & Grace* DVDs at the PX and watching them at your bunk, unafraid of being outed. Don't Ask Don't Tell—which will eventually be repealed—protects you.

Go to the makeshift gym on base. Lift weights with Fly. Feel that strange charge pulse through your body again and pretend, just for a moment, that you are that man from Kosovo again, the one who felt his gut flutter while watching Fly lift weights. When Fly reaches up and squeezes your shoulder after a good workout in that gym in Iraq, turn and look him in the eyes, but then quickly look away, as you've been conditioned to do, even though every part of you wants to grab him by the waist and pull him toward you.

7. Tell your friends and relatives how you'd like to celebrate.

At the airport, returning from Iraq, feel a wave of déjà vu wash over you as you take the escalator down to the mob of family and friends. Remember returning from Kosovo with your secret, how you were this fragile egg cracking open, ready to become something else. Wonder whether this man returning from Iraq feels the same. Shake away that wonder, the answer being obvious.

Stand at the bottom of the escalator and look for your mother's sign. Breathe a sigh of relief when you see her and realize that she doesn't have one this time.

Hug your mother. Shake your father's hand. Answer their questions about the flight, about the deployment, the feeling of being home. Look around at everyone else standing in little clumps. Notice the welcome back banners held overhead, the flowers handed between couples. Feel the relief of being home, surrounded by loved ones, on familiar ground again. Your enlistment is up, you will no longer be returning to drill in a couple months, so scan the crowd for Fly, because you must see him one last time. When you can't find him, take it as a sign that it's time to move on. Then grab your duffle and follow your parents back out into the world.

8. Limit your use of alcohol.

At a party, when a guy asks what you did in Iraq, tell him you killed twenty-seven Iraqis. Wait a beat to see if he believes you. Then chuckle to yourself and look at your hands. Don't tell him that it's only a joke to break the tension. Don't tell him what you really did in Iraq, that you poured cement, framed walls, and stood guard, that you stared at all the ashy sand and thought about your first boyfriend. You never fired your weapon or chambered a round or even aimed your rifle at another human being. But he doesn't need to know that. Let him believe you to be a killer.

Later, half-drunk, lie on your bed and feel regret at letting the guy think you did more than just pour concrete and stand guard in Iraq. Think about all the names for people who *steal valor* (fabricating or embellishing their service)—*military posers, fake warriors, medal cheats, Walts* (after Walter Mitty, in James Thurber's 1939 story, who daydreamed about being a war hero). Wonder about the ways you have felt like an imposter in the military, a spy moving between two worlds, and how this last lie was the worst and the most necessary. You needed to tell it to make yourself feel better about being a veteran, to make you feel like you actually earned this new title by killing someone over there.

In the morning, brush off the joke as the gesture of a young person not having the right words to talk about how he feels. Tell yourself that one day you will have the right words. One day you'll be ready.

9. Talk about how you're feeling.

When Tuna emails three months after returning from Iraq, saying he'll be in town and inviting you to dinner, say yes. Drive with anxious excitement to the restaurant. Remember how convivial it felt to serve and live with these men and how relieved you are to finally have someone to talk to about reintegrating into civilian life. Think about everything you have to say to them.

At the restaurant, shake hands with Tuna and several other men from your platoon. When they ask what you are doing, tell them about finishing college and applying to graduate school. Say how good it feels to not have to go to weekend drill. Ask them about the platoon: who left, who else has moved on. Ask them about new people and summer camp and future trainings. Don't even bring up Iraq. Don't tell them that you feel somewhat lost now that you aren't in the military. Don't tell them that the man you thought you were after the Kosovo deployment—the one who came out to his closest friends and cycled through a series of boyfriends yet hadn't yet come out to his family—was thinking about re-enlisting because it just felt easier than trying to figure out who he was all over again. Don't tell them that you just wish you had someone to say all of this to.

Instead, silently watch the men from your former unit as they cut up their steaks and swig their beers and let the conversation fall into awkward silence. In the parking lot, vow to stay in touch, even though you know you'll never see these men again.

10. Know when to seek help.

Dream about returning to Iraq. Recognize the smoke and the sand as definitively Iraq. Acknowledge that your biggest fear is having to go back. Instead of checking for accuracy, let your subconscious rewrite the narrative of your time in Iraq. Recreate the soldier you were. Replace the lazy, unmotivated, jaded man with someone more welcoming and accepting and grateful for what he did and did not do in Iraq. March this new soldier out of those dreams so he can help you cope with the feeling of being an undeserving veteran.

In the morning, construct imaginary emails to all the men and women you served with, asking whether they have these dreams, whether they still think about Iraq. Realize, again, that you have very few people to talk to about your time over there and, now that you are ready to talk about Iraq, you have no one to do it with.

Wonder what Fly thinks. Look him up on Facebook but don't send a friend request.

On the ten-year anniversary of returning from Iraq, write a real email to Leaf, one of only a few people from your platoon you are still in contact with. Ask if he wants to get a drink. Don't mention your dreams. Try not to come off as needy. When he accepts, arrange a time to meet at a bar in a city you used to live in. Spend the entire drive to that city thinking about what you want to say, what words to use, and how many beers you will need to help you talk.

When you arrive, belly up to the bar. Text your boyfriend. Listen to the jukebox playing *Hey Jealousy* by Gin Blossoms, *Hold My Hand* by Hootie & the Blowfish. Cherish the way the nineties music makes you feel, as if you are young and free and good. Finish your beer, order another. Check your phone. Text your boyfriend to say you think you are being stood up. Another beer. More nineties music. Remember how it felt to want to become someone else. To want to be seen and heard and understood. To connect with someone on a real, genuine level. This has become harder and harder the older you get. Look at all the other men and women sitting by themselves at the bar and wonder whether you'll ever find someone who truly sees you and understands how you feel. That is all you really want from this world.

Order another beer. Text your boyfriend again. Wait and wait and wait for a man who never arrives.

Sea Legs

On the morning before our scheduled swim call above the Mariana Trench—the deepest point in the world's oceans—my students asked me whether I was going to swim. I told them I wasn't sure.

Maybe, I said. *I haven't decided yet.*

I didn't tell them about my fear of the sea, how I didn't trust my swimming abilities in that much water, how I couldn't help but think about all that darkness extending down into that trench. I'd heard about swim calls before boarding the ship. I'd seen pictures of men and women jumping from the cargo hold of an aircraft carrier, diving into the crystal blue waters, bobbing around like beach balls. I hadn't heard whether anyone had ever died during a swim call, if anything had ever reached up and pulled anyone under. But I was convinced that that kind of thing happened all the time.

You should just do it, jump in, let yourself go, my students said, sensing my hesitation.

I told them I'd think about it.

I was onboard the USS *Chancellorsville*—a guided-missile cruiser ship, part of the U.S. Navy, where I had taken a job teaching—and I found the sea both terrifying and mysterious. Before boarding, I'd swum in an ocean only once, in high school, when I traveled to Oregon on a 4-H exchange trip and swam in the water near Haystack Rock. I did a lot of staring out at the sea during that trip, too. I stood along the shore and took pictures of the way Haystack Rock cast a shadow over the water, the way the sunlight rippled out across the sea, the way the water stretched on forever. Then, I put the camera down and slowly

walked into the water, gently stepping over the soft sand. When the
water was waist high, I turned and looked back, making sure the land
was still there.

Onboard the *Chancellorsville*, I was trying to turn into my fears, to
embrace them and not let them hold me back. *How else would I truly
find my way in this world if I wasn't willing to tackle my fears head on?* The
sea was a mystery to me, and, instead of turning my back on it, I always
kept it in mind, never knowing when something new would be revealed.

∼

Before boarding the *Chancellorsville*, I had rarely set foot on a boat. I
grew up in landlocked North Dakota—forty-five miles from a place
claiming to be the "geographic center of North America," the farthest
inland you could get. On the rare occasions I found myself on a boat, I
could always see land. Swatches of gangly trees or a brown riverbank.
Something to ground me, to make me feel stable and safe.

I took a job on a Navy ship then, not because of any interest or famil-
iarity with the sea but because I was looking for a new community. I
had just finished graduate school, where I'd spent three years immersed
in reading and discussing literature and writing. Most of my classmates
left after we graduated—to either explore new opportunities in new cities or to return to their hometowns—and since I didn't want to return
to North Dakota, I applied to any job that sounded interesting. I eventually accepted a position teaching an eight-week composition course
onboard a U.S. Navy ship as it sailed across the Pacific Ocean, hoping
the experience would help direct me toward a new community.

I flew to Hawaii to meet up with the ship. When I walked into the
belly of a Grumman C-2 Greyhound cargo plane, I was flooded with all
these memories from my time serving in the Army. The buckle of the
seat belt. The ear plugs. The smell of military canvas. It all made me
think back to the day I boarded a military plane on an airbase in Balad,
Iraq, and how excited and scared I was to leave, how a woman with the
flight crew stood near one of only two windows on the plane as I nervously clutched my M-16 and tried to look through the window over
her shoulder as we ascended in a spiral up and away from Iraq.

On the cargo plane, I thought about the men and women I'd be teaching on the Navy ship and how excited I was to be back in a military environment again. I'd served in the Army after high school, and even though I ultimately realized that the military wasn't the right fit for me, there were aspects I enjoyed about my time in the military. I liked the camaraderie and energy and the idea of being part of something bigger than myself. I liked being around a group of people driven by the sense of duty that came with serving their country.

But once I landed on the USS *Ronald Reagan* aircraft carrier, this nostalgic feeling changed. There was a vastness to the carrier that I wasn't prepared for. It was like wandering around a small, unfamiliar city. I got handed off to a public affairs representative who showed me where the MWR (Morale, Welfare, and Recreation) room was and where I'd be sleeping for the night and then disappeared. I got lost wandering the hallways. I was confused by all the pill-shaped doorways descending (it seemed) for eternity. I eventually found the MRW room and stayed there until dinnertime, when I went searching for the public affairs representative because I had no idea where to find food.

The next morning, I sat in the holding room below the flight deck, waiting to catch a helicopter out to the *Chancellorsville*, eighty textbooks next to me, wondering what I'd gotten myself into. I felt like a piece of freight waiting to be carted off. Someone leaned over and asked, "So, you're headed out to the small boy, huh?," and I nodded but didn't say anything because I wasn't sure what a "small boy" was.

On the helicopter ride, I looked out the side window at the sea. It swirled and bubbled and foamed. It spit up tiny geysers that splashed back down and dissolved into nothing. Every few feet, ominous, dark patches appeared, shadows that morphed and shifted with the tide. I watched these shadows and felt this creeping sense of unease run up my spine. In my mind, I saw this whole teeming ocean with creatures I'd seen only on TV—stingrays and hammerhead sharks and jellyfish—and with each bubble, I imagined something emerging, flipping itself around, and disappearing back into the darkness below. I tried to look away, first at the pilots, then at my hands, and finally at the bolts on the seat in front of me. But that didn't work. My eyes kept drifting back to the sea.

When I landed on the USS *Chancellorsville*, I wobbled a little bit stepping out of the helicopter, then steadied myself and followed the crew
into a hangar. Inside, I met Chief Plater, the education services officer
onboard. I stood next to him, smiling politely as my bag was unloaded
and placed next to me, but inside I was frantically trying to process
everything. My eyes were cataloging the contents of the hangar. My
ears were perked up and alert, listening to the whine of the ship and the
whipping of the helicopter blades. My legs were trying to find solid
footing, to keep me steady and still. As Chief Plater led me down a set
of stairs, the ship rocked a bit and I put my hands up against the walls
to steady myself. The sea was gently pushing the ship around, lapping
up against the hull, telling me it hadn't forgotten about me.

~

The floors were called decks. The hallways were passageways or
p-ways. The ceiling was referred to as "overhead." Stairs were ladders,
walls were bulkheads, doors between decks were hatches. Some of these
things I knew before boarding the ship; others I picked up.

The rooms were called compartments. There was a bridge, an engine
room, a post office. Storage rooms and staterooms and berthing areas
and heads. All the compartments were numbered according to a four-
digit code separated by hyphens. The first number referred to the decks
on the ship. The second had to do with the frame. The third number
was a reference to the ship's centerline, and the fourth number referred
to the compartment's function. I thought about these numbers and the
ship's imaginary centerline and how many decks there were on the
ship—no one ever told me—as I wandered down a p-way or took a ladder to an upper deck or stood in the center of a compartment and tried
to imagine whether I was above or below the tide. The numbers pro-
vided order to all the new information I was absorbing during the first
few days onboard the *Chancellorsville*.

My compartment was called the officer's overflow berthing area,
where they put the junior officers and civilians. There were twelve beds,
stacked in three-high bunks facing each other. Overhead, there were
two lights with three settings—white, red, and off. In the evenings,

after taps played, the white light was switched over to the red one, which cast a sharp hue around the room, making it feel as if you were swimming through blood.

My bed was called a rack. Sometimes the racks were called "coffin lockers" because when you lifted the bed there was storage underneath—places to put all your personal belongings. Sometimes, when I was tired of planning lessons or watching the sea from the weather deck, I'd stand in the aisle next to my rack, bed up, staring at my stuff, moving and rearranging where my socks or underwear were stored just for something to do. Other times, I'd lie on the thin mattress and stare at the rack above me. I'd pull the navy-blue curtain closed, click off the reading light, and just lie there in the dark, listening to the ship whine and wheeze. If the tide was strong enough, the ship would rock gently with the current, making it feel like I was actually in a coffin adrift on the dark and dangerous sea.

Eventually, I learned the different parts of the ship—stern, bow, hull, mast. I created a map of the ship in my head. I memorized which p-ways took me where—from my rack to the classroom, from my rack to the wardroom, from my rack to the weather deck where I stared out at the sea. I figured out which hatches took me outside, topside. I learned where I could be and where I couldn't. Most important, I learned to pay attention while out on the weather deck, that the flashing red lights meant a helicopter was about to land and I shouldn't walk around the stern end of the ship—as I had done a few days after coming onboard—unless I wanted to risk being blown into the sea.

～

I was onboard a week before anyone asked me about my sea legs.

I was in the wardroom listening to the officers complain. Two of them were having trouble sleeping. Their staterooms were right below the hangar bay, and they had been awakened in the middle of the night by helicopters landing and taking off and by the flight patrol team dragging chains across the floor of the bay.

"I kept hearing that sound in my head," the officer said. "The sound of chains being dragged across metal."

I ducked a little behind the menu I was holding, to keep the officers from seeing me chuckle to myself. Their conversation reminded me of the Flying Dutchman legend or *Pirates of the Caribbean*. I thought about all the different sea stories I'd heard over the year and the kind of spirits who haunted the different vessels. I wondered whether *Chancellorsville* had any stories to tell, whether eventually I'd bump into a ghost or two while out wandering the p-ways, whether they'd have anything of value to say about living at sea.

When the officers were finished complaining, they turned to me.

"Have you found your sea legs yet?" one of the officers asked me after I placed my breakfast order with the wardroom attendant and handed over the menu.

I smiled at the officers, unsure of what to say.

"I haven't fallen down yet," I replied, hopefully.

I didn't tell them that I enjoyed hearing them complain because it made me feel better about my own difficulties adjusting to life onboard. I also didn't reveal that I still walked the p-ways with my hands braced against the bulkheads, that a few days ago I had been thrown into the bulkhead outside my berthing area by the rough rocking of the ship and had leaned against the wall and waited for several minutes until I felt like moving again.

"That's part of it," another officer said, still looking at his menu.

He didn't tell me what the other part was.

Getting your sea legs, I later learned, meant more than just being able to walk onboard a ship while at sea. It meant acclimating to your surroundings and becoming comfortable with your environment. It meant finding balance with the sea, a sort of agreement where you submitted to the great, roiling water and in return the sea showed you the wonders it holds.

It seemed like a fair trade-off to me at the time, this wandering soul looking for a little adventure.

~

On the day before my class began, Chief Plater arranged two hours for me to meet my students and sell textbooks in the classroom. As students entered the room, I introduced myself, shook their hands, gave them their textbooks, and collected information for payment. Most then turned and left. A few students stayed and asked whether I was finding my way around the ship all right. I smiled back at them and explained that I was still adjusting, still trying to figure out how to feel steady while onboard. In return, I asked the students who stayed what they did on the ship.

"Machinery repairman," one student said. "I work in the deepest part of the ship."

"Ah," I said, raising my brow. "Do you like it?"

"Yes and no," he said. "Somedays I do. Some days I don't."

The student's name was Henderson. He was older than most of the other students, with close-cropped hair and a thin mustache above his lip.

"My wife encouraged me to take this class," Henderson said. "To get an education. To move up."

I nodded and smiled. I liked Henderson. There was something genuine and down-to-earth about him. He reminded me of some of the men from the engineering unit I had been part of in the Army. Approachable, honest, willing to share something about themselves if you are willing to listen.

On my way back to my rack, I stopped above the ladder leading down into the belly of the ship. I stared down into the semidarkness below, remembering what Henderson had said about working in the deepest part of the ship. I had no sense of how many decks were on the *Chancellorsville*. The computer room was at the bottom of the ladder, but I didn't know what else was down there. I pictured one of those illustrations I saw online, where the hull was transparent so you could see everything inside. I imagined sailors typing emails to loved ones back home or playing games on the computers. I imagined a deck with fuel storage and machinery compartments and, below that, an even deeper deck, the deepest one on the ship, barely big enough for a person to stand in. That was where I pictured Henderson, standing among the missiles, thinking about his wife, his children, maybe even thinking about my class. I shivered a little bit thinking about him down so deep, next to the missiles, the ship's hull the only thing protecting him from the wild and cold sea full of who-knows-what. *Did he feel comfortable there, down so deep, tucked away where so many could forget about him?*

I wanted to step down that ladder into the lower decks, but I couldn't get my feet to make that move. The deeper you were on the ship, I felt, the harder it would be to climb to the surface and shake the grip the sea had on you.

～

I was out on the weather deck watching the sea, thinking about how easy it would be for me to fall overboard (What would it take? A strong wind? A wet deck? A blast of hot air from a landing helicopter? And if I did fall overboard, what would happen? Would anyone even know I was gone?) when I noticed a burial at sea ceremony on the fantail of the ship.

The fantail was the very back part of the ship. Historically, it was where sailors would go to goof off or blow off steam, sort of like the back porch of the ship. They told jokes. They talked about their wives and girlfriends back home. They spread rumors. They tried to forget about their work, that they were on a warship, that they were millions of miles away from land and the ones they loved. Most Sundays, when the weather was nice, the *Chancellorsville* hosted "Steel Beach Picnics" on the fantail. They hauled out a grill and a boombox and allowed the men and women to mill about the fantail as if they were at a park. People still told jokes and complained and tried to forget about their jobs on the ship.

I stood at the edge of the fantail, under a giant American flag whipping around at half-mast, watching a chaplain speak into a microphone. At the very back of the fantail was a stand with an urn on top. Next to it was a podium, and off to one side of the fantail was a line of men with rifles. I listened to a chaplain say a few prayers, and then I heard a bagpipes version of "Amazing Grace" come through the portable speakers. Just then, Chief Plater stepped up next to me.

"Retired Navy," he said without looking at me, answering my unspoken question about who was in the urn. "Being returned to the sea."

He said this last part with a wistful sadness that made me think about how we return to the things we love but also how sometimes we're drawn back to things we don't understand, for reasons we can't explain. I felt this way taking the job with the Navy, an institution I didn't understand but knew held some of the same core values as the Army I had been a part of when I was younger.

When "Amazing Grace" ended, one of the sailors took the urn from the stand and tipped the contents overboard.

~

The night before our first liberty port in Hong Kong, I woke up screaming in the middle of the night. I pulled back the blue curtain into my coffin-rack and said, *"Can't breathe."* One of my roommates—a junior officer—asked if I was all right. I didn't reply.

We were in the wardroom having breakfast the next morning when my roommate asked me about the screaming.

"Sorry," I said. "That sometimes happens to me in unfamiliar places. I get a little claustrophobic."

I looked down into my breakfast, slightly ashamed. After being onboard twenty-two days, I thought I'd gotten used to a few things, like sleeping in my rack, but with this dream my subconscious was telling me that I hadn't yet found my sea legs. I was still a little wobbly, still a little unsure of so much around me.

After breakfast, I went topside to watch as we approached Hong Kong Island. I stood on the starboard side of the ship, near the bow, and stared at the approaching land. It was the first land I'd seen since leaving Hawaii and flying to the USS *Ronald Reagan*. At first there were only slivers on the horizon, uninhabitable hills of indistinguishable greens and browns. But, as we got closer to Hong Kong, I could make out the rocky beaches and the windows of buildings built into the sides of hills and roads that snaked along the coast. Eventually, the skyscrapers came into view, first the tips poking out from behind the hills, then the full view of all those tall buildings right down by the water, column after column crammed together at the foot of a dark and looming mountain.

We had three days of shore leave in Hong Kong, so once I set foot on dry land again, I tried to do as much as I could during this time. I took the tram to Victoria Peak, hiked around the park, took pictures of myself with the skyscrapers of Hong Kong behind my right shoulder. I then took the ferry across Victoria Harbor and spent all afternoon in the air-conditioned Hong Kong Museum of History, soaking up as much history about the city as I could. In the late afternoon, I caught a ferry out to Lantau Island to see the Tian Tan Buddha. I climbed all 268 steps, my legs burning from not using them much during my twenty-two days on the *Chancellorsville*. That evening, I could have slept in a hotel in Hong Kong, away from the ship and the coffin-rack I'd found suffocating the night before, but after a day of unfamiliar sights and sounds, I wanted to be back where everything felt at least somewhat familiar, and the ship had started to feel that way to me. I knew what to expect on the ship. I'd gotten used to the way it rocked and swayed. It didn't yet feel like home, but I liked it better than a cold hotel room. Plus, I was still working on turning into my fears and the only way to combat waking up screaming was to try to make the place I slept feel less and less like a suffocating coffin.

So, I caught a speedboat back to the *Chancellorsville*—smiling as we zipped past all the skyscrapers lit up and sparkling like jewels—and once onboard, I climbed into my rack, pulled that familiar blue curtain closed, and sealed myself back into my coffin.

~

Something changed after that first shore leave in Hong Kong. Having wandered a foreign land and stretched my legs a bit, I felt differently about the ship and my place upon it. Whereas Hong Kong felt vast and impersonal while I was wandering around it, the ship felt comfortable, safe, familiar. The things I once found annoying—like the constant instructions and announcements blasted from the speaker system at all hours of the day, first with directions to "heave out and trice up" and later in the day with calls to flight quarters ("Flight Quarters! Flight Quarters! Set condition 1-alpha for flight operations!") and a loud, drawn-out "CLAMPDOOOOOWN!," which I think had something to do with cleaning—now felt like rallying cries I felt obliged to get behind (even though I didn't know what most of the announcements meant). My very sense of being on the ship had shifted.

I felt this shift most prominently in the evenings. I used to ignore the evening announcements, but after Hong Kong, I found them kind of comforting. I was usually reading in my rack when the "Tattoo, Tattoo. Stand by for evening prayer" announcement came through the speakers at five minutes to ten at night. The announcement usually began with a story or joke. Sometimes the story was overly patriotic or just plain schmaltzy. Other times it struck the perfect balance of sentiment and insight. After the story came the prayer, which was the same every night. It asked God to look over those on watch, to give rest to tired eyes, and to keep everyone safe and together and well. The guy who made the announcement was always the same, and he had a voice perfect for soothing people to sleep. It made me feel that he was talking directly to me, and, lying on my rack with my eyes closed, I felt that I was actually part of the ship, part of the team of men and women onboard. I wasn't integral to the operation of the ship, but I felt as if I had a small part to play onboard.

The problem came then during the shore leaves. I had become so comfortable with my new state of being on the ship that I didn't know what to do with myself during the shore leaves. I didn't have any plans for our second shore leave in Guam, and since I still felt like a bit of an outsider among the men and women onboard, I thought it would be weird following them around Guam like a lost dog. So, when we docked, I waited in my rack for thirty minutes, for everyone to leave, then grabbed my backpack and wandered off to explore the island alone.

By the time we docked for our third shore leave in Busan, South Korea—two weeks after visiting Guam—I was broke (I didn't get paid for teaching until after the class was finished) and tired of wandering around foreign places alone. Instead of going topside to watch as we pulled into port, I climbed into my rack, pulled the curtain closed, and waited for everyone to leave the ship.

The ship wasn't completely empty. Some personnel were required to stay onboard. But it was noticeably quieter than when we were at sea.

For two days, I stayed onboard while almost everyone else explored South Korea. I graded papers and listened to music. I ate whatever geedunk and junk food I could scrounge up without having to go to the wardroom. I went down those steps I'd stopped at before and scavenged through a couple boxes of books and then took a few back to my rack and spent hours reading there. I hadn't been entirely alone in nearly two months, so I cherished the time to myself. But after the second night, melancholy set in. I felt this hollowness when I wandered the p-ways and didn't see a single soul. I found that I missed being at sea. I missed the daily hum of activity, the routine I'd developed after being onboard for so many weeks. I missed the announcements and the constant noise and the gentle rock and sway of the ship. After a couple of days at port, I found myself longing for us to set sail again, to get back to our journey, to return to what had become familiar.

Somehow the sea had tricked me into missing it.

~

I shouldn't have been afraid of the sea. The sea could cause harm, for sure, but while I was on the *Chancellorsville*, it did nothing but enchant me with its glittering water and mesmerizing waves. It was just a distraction to get me thinking about something other than how terribly lonely and out of place I felt in the world. There was much more danger in the things that floated *on* the sea than in the sea itself.

As my students' last readings, I assigned two essays about torture. Both essays had been published two months after the 9/11 attacks. One advocated bringing back torture. The other called torture an "absolute evil." I wanted to use these opposing viewpoints to discuss argumentative writing, but I also wanted to see whether the students had gleaned any insights from serving on a Navy warship.

After the discussion of the essays, I launched into the final writing assignment—to make an argument for something as an "absolute evil." The students could write about a serious topic like racism or torture—both topics we discussed in class—or they could write about a humorous topic like dating or self-driving cars. I asked them to take out some paper and start brainstorming ideas, and after a few minutes, I started making my way around the room, pausing to ask each student about his or her ideas for this final essay. Near the end of my loop around the room, I stopped next to the desk of one student, a woman who had been silent for most of our discussion about torture.

"Did you come up with an absolute evil?" I asked.

The student nodded.

"Homosexuals," she said. "Homosexuals are an absolute evil."

I had never told any of my students that I was gay. Still, I was surprised by how absolute my student was, how sure of herself and her beliefs, how positive she was that homosexuals weren't just bad or sinful, but an *absolute* evil. And I was surprised that she felt comfortable saying that to me, a man she'd known for only a few short weeks, a man who shared a little bit about his life and service in the military in order to make her and the other students feel more comfortable with him but who didn't share everything—like his sexuality.

She was looking up at me, waiting for my reaction, and thinking quickly, I asked what other ideas she'd written down. Her comment had me feeling a little less comfortable with my place on the ship, but I was still upright. The sea legs I'd developed over the eight weeks I'd been onboard were keeping me standing and preventing me from toppling overboard.

∽

When I got to the weather deck on the day of the swim call, there was already a line of people waiting to jump in. Men in shorts, a few in T-shirts. Women in swimsuits and wrapped in towels. They inched forward, and once at the edge of the fantail, they jumped into the sea. Some alone, some in pairs. I watched them fall from the side of the *Chancellorsville*—feet pointed, arms dangling, thundering torsos splashing into the water. They swam away from the ship, to the starboard side, where others were bobbing and floating and splashing around. When they'd had enough, they swam over to the cargo net dangling off the side of the ship and climbed out of the water.

Beyond the swimmers were two patrol boats, each with a man holding a gun.

"What's with the guns?" I asked the guy standing next to me.

"To scare away sharks," the guy said.

I want that job, I thought, briefly, knowing it would never happen because they would never be able to get me into one of those tiny patrol boats. I just liked the idea of shooting sharks.

"Are there sharks often?" I asked.

The guy shrugged.

I watched the swimmers laughing and smiling and having fun, and I tried to convince myself to get in line. I tried to listen to my students and just let all my fears about the sea drift away. *Fuck it*, I told myself. *Just do it. Maybe swimming will help curb this fear of the sea and all the things below the surface. Maybe splashing around will prepare me for when I inevitably fall overboard.* It was a once-in-a-lifetime opportunity to swim in the deepest part of any ocean, and I didn't want to regret not taking it. But then my eyes wandered away from the swimmers and the patrol boats and focused on the calm water beyond the swim call area. The water stretched in all directions, all the way to the horizon, and watching it I was paralyzed by the vastness of it all. All I could think about was the darkness, the depth, and everything lurking below. All the unknown.

I stood there holding the railing, watching as men and women climbed back onboard, laughing, dripping, satisfied. Safe. But I couldn't make myself let go of that railing and step in line. I just couldn't submit to the sea.

Two weeks later, I entered the wardroom and heard the officers chatting about a crack in the hull of the ship. After asking permission to join them (wardroom etiquette dictates that if you arrive late to a meal, you must ask the captain or most senior officer to join the mess table), I looked over the POD (Plan of the Day) and noticed an announcement about something being wrong with the fuel storage on the ship and how we needed to dock to get it fixed.

The POD said we shouldn't worry. Still, I couldn't help thinking about the crack. All through breakfast, and into the morning, I kept thinking about the crack spreading, getting wider, bigger, spiderwebbing out across the entire hull. I remembered back to the day before class, when Henderson said, "I work in the deepest part of the ship," and how I froze above the ladder to the computer room, imagining the decks below, all the different transparent layers of the ship. In my mind, the crack started in that deepest part of the ship and slowly inched up and up and up, deck by deck. It crept down the p-ways and branched out across the compartments, knocked over tables, pulled back curtains, snatched all the geedunk it could find. It turned into this living, breathing thing that wouldn't stop until it found what it was looking for.

I hadn't accepted the sea's invitation during swim call, so, instead, the sea was coming for me.

Stalactites

I celebrated my first week as an expat in China at a bar called American Pie. The walls were painted orange, and a string of plastic American flags ran the length of the bar. There were a dozen photographs of American landmarks randomly plastered to one wall. The Statue of Liberty. The Grand Canyon. The Rocky Mountains. Patrons had written messages in black Sharpie around these photographs, a record of foreigners passing through. I signed my name next to a photograph of the Golden Gate Bridge, then lifted a bottle of local beer. *To new opportunities*, my new colleague said. I clanged my bottle against his. *To China,* I replied.

I'd moved to China because I needed a job and teaching English composition to Chinese college students sounded like an adventure. I knew very little about China when I left the U.S., only a handful of facts from history classes and the things I'd glimpsed while watching the 2008 Olympic Games in my brother's living room in North Dakota. I expected paper lanterns, slippery dumplings, three-wheeled tuk-tuks, and smog. I expected old men playing mah-jongg and cute schoolchildren smiling and jumping and waving tiny Chinese flags (like the kids on the cover of my guidebook). I expected old cities with protective dragon statues at the entrances and giant pictures of Mao and a crumbling wall you could see from outer space. I knew these were stereotypes of China, but I found them both comforting and seductive.

A few weeks after my first visit, I tried to go back to the American Pie bar, to ground myself and remind myself of home, but when I got there the doors were boarded up, the lights out, the wall of names that seemed like it would always be there gone. It was as if the bar had never even existed, almost as if I'd made the whole place up. I paced the sidewalk outside the bar, wondering what to do. I needed *something* else to latch onto, to remind me of where I'd come from. Without that grounding, I was afraid of getting lost in all the glittering novelty of being in a new country, of drifting along untethered.

~

When I first arrived in the country, I wanted to spend all my weekends exploring as much of the country as I could. But all the major sights— Tiananmen Square, the Forbidden City, the Great Wall—were too far away (I was living near the northeast corner of China, away from the major cities and tourist attractions), and I was still too inexperienced with the country and its people, so the teachers I was working with suggested I start out with a day trip to somewhere nearby. I took the train to Benxi, thirty-five miles south of where I was living, and then a three-hour bus ride into the mountains, to a park with an underground river and a series of caves with stalactites and stalagmites.

Outside the Benxi Water Caves, I noticed a statue of a melting elephant on red marble tiles near the entrance. I approached the statue from behind, where it just looked like a rock, but as I moved around to the side the elephant materialized. I saw the hump in the middle of the back, the dinner-plate-size feet, the craggy ears, the trunk half-submerged in the tiles. The elephant was slate gray near the bottom but chalky white at the top with streaks of pale yellow all the way down the trunk and off the back haunches. It was a man-made sculpture meant to look like a stalagmite rising from the ground. When I visited in September 2008, all I saw was an animal going the other way, melting as if corrosive acid were eating away its flesh. It reminded me of that scene from *Dumbo*, where the mother elephant is shackled inside the trailer crying. I still can't watch it without a few tears pooling in the corners of my eyes.

I stared at the melting elephant and thought about extinction and separation and ice cream dripping off a sugar cone on a hot summer day. Then I reached out and touched its ear. I knew it wasn't real stone—it looked like that newer plastic garden gnomes are made of— but I had to be sure. It felt rough and sandpapery. I ran my hand over the melting elephant's forehead and down its trunk. Behind me, a group of tourists shuffled toward the mouth of the caves, their excited chatter echoing off the mountainside.

Beyond the melting elephant was a man-made pond with a stone path across the middle, willows around the edges, and a pagoda on the far bank. It was a warm autumn day when I visited, and the leaves on the willows were bright orange and yellow. The lily pads scattered across the pond seemed to sparkle. It all felt very magical, just the way I'd imagined China would feel.

My guidebook made the forty-five-minute boat ride through the Benxi Water Caves sound like a carnival ride. The entry—under the sub- heading "Around Shenyang"—described a trip along a river called the Milky Way, where stalactites and stalagmites were spotlighted with red or green or blue lights and given names to signify what they looked like—Seal Playing with a Pearl, Tiger's Mouth, Ginseng Baby. Riding along the Milky Way felt like being on a movie set. The evocative names given to the formations were fun because they made you use your imag- ination to see the image in the rock.

Outside the caves, I saw the China I had been looking forward to, with the pond and pagoda and willow trees and tourists. But the guide- book and the melting elephant had primed me for a different experience inside the caves—one of make-believe, where imaginations conjured up images from rock, where visitors were asked to see what those before them had already identified and named, a manufactured experience created to make the real seem more exciting. This was why I'd come to the caves—to find a connection with the country I'd come so far to see. I was aimless, drifting, waiting for something to snag my collar and hold me in place. And, as foolish and hopeful as it sounds, I thought floating down an underground river and conjuring up the images assigned to the stalactites and stalagmites would show me something real about China, not just this place I'd cobbled together in my head.

There are clues hidden below the surface, I thought. I hoped to see what everyone else saw, that I wouldn't look at all the named stalactites and stalagmites and just see rock.

Next to the melting elephant was a metal sign claiming—in white English letters below the Chinese characters—that the Milky Way river was "the longest underground river in the world." This claim wasn't in my guidebook, so I didn't know what to make of it. I knew the Chinese government liked to exaggerate, to make things seem better than they actually were. But I wanted to believe that the claim was true—that I *was* about to float down the longest underground river in the world— and that meant tamping down my tendency to question everything. I knew that if I weren't open to what I was experiencing I wouldn't last very long in China. So, I snapped a picture of the sign, and as I walked toward the mouth of the caves, I gave myself permission to believe.

~

When we were in graduate school, my friend Natalie and I played this game where we'd guess what the other saw in everyday objects. We didn't have a name for the game, or maybe we did and I just don't remember it or we never vocalized it while we were playing, but it was a game we took pride in playing because we liked to think we saw the world the same way.

One of us would hold up an object or point at something and simply say, *Do you see it?* A typical exchange went something like this:

"Do you see it?" Natalie would say, holding a chicken nugget out before me.

I'd glance up from the hamburger I was eating, see the rubber ducky shape in the chicken nugget, and smile.

"It's a rubber ducky," I'd say.

She'd smile back at me, satisfied.

Then she'd bite off the rubber ducky's head.

I don't know why we found so much pleasure in this game. Maybe it reminded us of childhood, when we'd stare at the clouds and point out the different shapes and ask our siblings or our friends whether they saw what we saw in the clouds. Maybe we liked the game because we both pointed at clouds into adulthood, unlike our friend Cat, who would shake her head at us when she saw us playing the game and half-scream, "It's a chicken nugget. A fucking chicken nugget!" We'd smile back at Cat, shake our heads, say, "Oh, Cat," and tsk-tsk at her lack of imagination.

Maybe we just needed to know someone else saw the world the same way we did.

When the whole *What color is the dress?* debate came up and people were discussing perception and "color constancy" and how our eyes aren't really seeing the world as it is, I thought of Natalie and wondered whether she found the whole debate as fascinating as I did, whether she saw the dress as white and gold or blue and black. I thought of her again when I found the "Faces in Things" Twitter feed and scrolled through pics of smiling faces with button eyes and zipper mouths, faces made from the knobs of appliances, faces made from the holes on cardboard boxes or soap bubbles. With each picture, I imagined Natalie being just as delighted by seeing the image as I was.

Later, I learned that there is a name for our ability to see hidden faces in random patterns—pareidolia. People see faces on the moon, faces on grilled cheese sandwiches, faces in clouds and trees and ocean waves. People see faces everywhere. Researchers have hypothesized that pareidolia is the result of natural selection, where people had to quickly identify the mental state or moods of others in order to survive. I smiled when I read this and imagined Natalie and me surviving into old age while Cat got killed by a lion or a band of angry savages.

I started playing the game with Natalie as a way to bond over our shared view of the world, but the game evolved beyond that. It became a survival mechanism I used any time I was faced with the unfamiliar; I'd turn it into something familiar, something others would also be able to see. If I could quickly assess new information and determine whether or not it was a threat, I might feel better about venturing into the unknown.

～

At first, China didn't feel like a threat. It felt strange and novel and raw. On one of my first walks from my apartment to campus, I cataloged all the sights of my new neighborhood, as a way of acclimating to my new environment. I passed old men sipping porridge from ceramic bowls while sitting on wooden chairs outside the front gate to my apartment complex. I watched sleepy teenagers tumble out of cyber cafes and drift off to class. Toddlers with slits in their trousers squatted and peed directly onto the sidewalk. Middle-aged men wandered around outside the cafes with their shirts rolled up to expose their bellies, smoking and talking loudly into cell phones. I observed it all with the moon-eyed naiveté of being in a new and foreign place, never questioning what I was seeing, simply letting the images come at me one after another and storing them away in my memory. Everything seemed just familiar enough to be relatable, yet foreign enough to be intriguing.

On subsequent walks, I started to connect what I was seeing to what I knew from back home. The old men reminded me of the farmers in the cafe in my hometown. The blurry-eyed teens stumbling out of a cyber cafe were just drunk college kids leaving bars. The tottering infants with split pants were like tiny dogs tagging what they could with urine. And the loud men with their exposed bellies were practical businessmen trying to stay cool while taking calls from important investors. I accepted these sights as part of my new normal. I liked to believe that I was becoming less like a tourist observing a place from the fringes and more like a real, integrated citizen. It felt safe, manageable. This series of unconnected pieces had started to fit together into a larger whole, making me feel like I could not only survive in China but maybe make a life for myself there.

～

I had wanted to drift down the Milky Way river inside the Benxi Water Caves and let the galaxy of stalactites and stalagmites present themselves around me—like an astronaut mindlessly floating through the void—but my own curiosity and need to create meaning from the unknown wouldn't let me be a passive passenger. I sat up, leaned slightly over the side of the boat, and analyzed the English words below the Mandarin on the little signs, trying to make out what I was supposed to see in the rock formations.

I saw "Lotus Coming out of Water" just above the tide, in a low cavern lit by green lights. I saw "Buddha's Hand" as we came around the bend of the river, and I watched as several passengers of my boat reached up and touched the hand. But somewhere around the third bend, I started to lose track. Things started to blur together. I saw the sign for the "Ginseng Baby" but I didn't see the baby. I also didn't see "Tail of Phoenix" or "Jade Emperor Palace." The boat was moving too fast. I couldn't take it all in. I couldn't sit and stare to see everything I needed to see.

Beyond feeling embarrassed, I started to doubt my ability to adapt to my surroundings. I felt I'd done a good job setting up my new life in China, establishing my surroundings and navigating some of the social cues I was noticing around me. But there were bigger issues I was just starting to see, and I wasn't prepared for the uncertainty of digging a little deeper into the culture and people around me. I looked at the sign for a stalactite named "Baoding Double Bells"—not sure what "Baoding" referred to but expecting my brain to come back with some image to latch onto—but instead I drew a blank. Nothing. There was something I was missing, something I wasn't picking up, something I couldn't quite explain, and this something created this sense of discomfort in the pit of my stomach that I wasn't sure what to do about.

∼

Over the course of several weeks, I developed this low-grade anxiety about everything in China. It started off with the simple and mundane but later spread to other aspects of my life. I stared at a patch of mold growing in the corner of my second bedroom, and, instead of contacting someone about it, I just closed the door and pretended it wasn't there. When it came time to get a haircut, I just let the stylist do what he wanted because I didn't know how to explain the way I liked it cut. The resulting haircuts didn't look much different from my normal cut, just slightly off and a little more "basic" than how I normally cut it. I constantly worried that I was being ripped off by shop owners and fruit sellers at the market, that I was paying more than anyone else because I was a foreigner. I fretted over counting money out in front of tellers, usually opting to give the teller a larger bill than necessary because I didn't know how much anything was supposed to cost. When I was shopping at Tesco down the street from my apartment, I didn't know how to tell the people around me to stop watching me, to mind their own business, to stop peering into my cart to see what the foreigner was buying. These anxieties made me question everything, to second-guess myself, to make me doubt my own abilities to adapt, and I hated this feeling of constantly being on guard. I thought my survival mechanism of creating meaning from the unknown would eventually kick in and squelch these anxieties, but the anxieties only got worse. Instead of making me more independent and resourceful, my survival mechanism turned me into a skeptic. I started to question everything about what I was seeing. *Was any of it real?* I started to wonder. *Or had I just created my own reality in order to mask my own insecurities about not being able to adjust to life in a foreign country?*

~

Near the end of the Milky Way river, before we turned around and headed back the way we came, I saw the image I'd been prepped to see—the melting elephant. Unlike the fake statue outside the cave, I saw this elephant right away. It was attached to the wall of the cave near its head, and the legs and trunk extended down into the river. We approached it from behind, which made it look as if we were sneaking up on it during bath-time. As we floated past, all the features came into view—the trunk, the ears, the rounded back, the half-squinting eye—and the sign confirmed what I was seeing—"Jade Elephant Playing in Water."

Finally, something I recognized.

When we got back to the entrance of the cave, I carefully stepped onto the dock and started walking down the hillside to see the crocodile taming show. I had heard about the show from a poorly translated website that described it as "the most exciting crocodile taming show in China." There were regular performances with crocodiles, the website claimed, "including playing with it and kissing it and so on," and since the ride through the caves left me questioning my ability to create meaning from the unknown, I wanted one last chance to redeem myself.

When I arrived at the arena, a woman was singing into a microphone while gesturing wildly with her free hand. Her face was stark white, her lips bold red. She wore a black sparkling dress with a slit up the front and high heels. Six feet away, a pale crocodile watched motionless on the concrete stage.

At first, I thought the woman was a drag queen because I'd heard about men performing female roles in Chinese opera and because I was familiar with drag queens back home. But the longer she sang and the more I watched her, I started to wonder if she was trans. I knew almost nothing about being trans in China, only that other foreigners called these women "ladyboys," both in China and in other Asian countries. I didn't know then any of the other terms used to describe trans people in China, such as the names I later discovered that literally translated to "human monster" or "human ghost."

After the performance, I walked down the road toward the entrance of the park, to catch my bus back to Shenyang. Another performer was standing in the doorway of a shed, shirtless but still "in-face," slightly out of view. I was thinking about the melting elephant and the limp crocodile and everything I had and hadn't seen during my visit. Before the performer dipped back into the darkness of the shed, before I caught the bus back to Benxi and the train back Shenyang, before spending two years trying to understand my students and the Chinese people and the country I'd dropped myself into, I caught the performer's eye and held it for a moment, unsure of so much around me yet hoping that the fog would lift and all the stalactites would present themselves to me eventually.

The fog lifted eventually, years later, when I found a map of the Milky Way river online, with the names and pictures of many of the rock formations along the route, and I paid a service to translate the map. As I had expected, there *was* a whole world below the surface—one that told stories about the Chinese people and their history—one I didn't see while I floated through the caves. There was a trio of lotus-themed formations near the entrance of the caves—not just the one I saw during my visit—followed by a trio of sword-themed formations. The melting elephant wasn't the only animal in the caves. There was also "Cicadas Playing in Water," "Crocodile Head," "Beetle Rock," and "Lying Cattle Looking Back," none of which I had seen when I visited. Then there were a series of formations whose names I didn't understand and had to look up—"Two Immortals' Palace," a reference to mountain-dwelling Taoists who strived for immortality, and "Rock of Weaving Girl," named for a Chinese folktale called "The Weaver Girl and the Cowherd," which is a love story about Zhinu (the weaver girl symbolizing the star Vega) and Niulang (the cowherd symbolizing the star Altair). I loved reading the names and learning about Chinese history and folklore, but, looking at the map and the translated names, I realized how very little I knew about the history and culture of China. The Benxi Water Caves showed me pieces of Chinese history and culture, placed them before me on little signs, and said *Do you see it?*, and I blinked back and shook my head.

In those first few months in China, I needed to see the familiar, to recognize something about the place where I'd decided to live and work because I thought it would help me understand China better but also because I'd wanted to see whether I had a future in China, whether I belonged there. Looking back on my time in China now, years later, in an old house I've settled into with my husband, I wish I could have let go of that need to understand everything around me. I wish I could have just admired the stalactites and stalagmites for their own beauty and not tried to see the images the signs told me I needed to see. I may have enjoyed my time in China more and not gotten burnt out on the country and its people after a couple of years.

Who Doesn't

I went to China with a romantic notion of expatriate life. It started in high school when I watched the movie *City of Angels*. In one scene, Nicholas Cage's creepy angel character tries to seduce Meg Ryan's character by reading a line about oysters from Hemingway's *A Moveable Feast*: "As I ate the oysters with their strong taste of the sea and their faint metallic taste that the cold white wine washed away, leaving only the sea taste and the succulent texture, and as I drank their cold liquid from each shell and washed it down with the crisp taste of the wine, I lost the empty feeling and began to be happy." I had never eaten oysters, never read Hemingway before seeing *City of Angels*, never felt this "empty feeling" he was talking about. But I liked the way the passage sounded, and I liked the idea that something so simple could take someone from emptiness all the way to happiness. So, I went looking for the book.

I found *A Moveable Feast* in a B. Dalton bookstore in the mall in Minot, North Dakota, and frantically read it in my basement bedroom back home. I liked going along with Hemingway on his walks through Paris—along the Seine and through the courtyards and down the narrow alleyways with all the old, beautiful houses. I loved reading all the French street names—rue de Fleurus, rue de l'Odéon, Boulevard St.-Germain—even though I didn't know how to pronounce any of them. I imagined Gertrude Stein in her Paris apartment—all the walls filled with abstract paintings in ornate frames—and the fancy salons she hosted, where foreigners met and mingled and talked about literary things. My favorite parts were the descriptions of the cafés—La Closerie des Lilas, Le Dôme—and all the artists and writers sitting around sipping *café crèmes* and sopping up sauce with crusty bread. I read right past all the "empty feeling" stuff the first time. Only later, re-reading the book in college, did I realize how lonely and isolating being an expatriate can be. They are surrounded by all this beauty, but deep down they feel empty and unsatisfied because they haven't found that thing—their oysters—that makes them happy.

After graduate school, and after teaching onboard a U.S. Navy ship for eight weeks, I got a job teaching at a university in the northeastern city of Shenyang. The university rented me an apartment just north of campus, and once I was handed the keys, I started putting together the expatriate life I'd imagined for myself after reading *A Moveable Feast*. I located the nearest friendly café, learned the Mandarin words for beer and my favorite dishes, and started cultivating friendships with the people I worked with. The week before Halloween, I hosted the foreign faculty in my apartment for a little "salon" of my own. I made brownies from a box mix I bought at Tesco and bought a variety of beers from the shop on the corner. On the walls, I hung two propaganda posters of Mao Zedong I'd found at an antique market near the Shenyang Imperial Palace. When everyone arrived, I showed them the pictures of shirtless Asian heartthrobs the previous occupant had taped inside my armoire. Later, we all crowded around my laptop to watch a pirated copy of *It's the Great Pumpkin, Charlie Brown*. It was a far cry from what I imagined Gertrude Stein's Paris salons to be like, but it was something. A beginning.

The party was an opportunity to get to know other expats. There was Heather, a creative writer from Baltimore who had briefly lived and worked in Kurdistan. There was Ryan, a goofy Midwesterner with a laugh like the Cowardly Lion from *The Wizard of Oz*. Then there was Lynda, a short, dark-haired woman from Vermont. During our first few weeks in China, I learned a lot about Lynda, and I knew we'd get along. She was personable, had a dry sense of humor, and loved to gossip. We'd often talk about writing and traveling and which foreign faculty were trying to hook up with Chinese women. If I imagined myself Hemingway in those days, she was my Sylvia Beach—the owner of the bookstore Hemingway frequented. She was a bit of a guide, and I quickly developed a fondness for the way she approached life and the hunger that kept her searching for more.

~

I didn't tell anyone about the real reason I came to China: because I didn't know where I belonged. I felt adrift and directionless, needy to find a home. Reading Hemingway in high school had helped me realize how out of place I was back in North Dakota. I was bored by the end-less prairie and snowbanks and all the farm machinery I'd see in the fields. I couldn't picture myself there, riding a combine through a field of North Dakota wheat or herding cattle across a wide-open pasture or even doing a job I loved. I just didn't feel that it was a place I could be myself in, unlike my five siblings, who all found jobs, got married, and settled down in the state. So, I left and started looking for something else. I thought maybe that place could be China.

During our first month in China, we stuck to our apartments and didn't venture out too far. We smoked on Ryan's rooftop balcony and watched paper lanterns drift over the campus buildings. In Lynda's liv-ing room, we listened to the music coming from her laptop speakers and talked about how oddly fascinated we were with our students. At Heather's, we discussed other foreigners we'd met and speculated about what made them stay in China. Often, we invited new people, other lonely foreigners looking for connection—Dan, an American teaching "oral English," or Paul, a lanky Frenchman who worked at our univer-sity. There was always beer—Tsingtao and Snow beer and whatever else we could find in glass bottles at the little shops at the corners of our apartment buildings—and usually whatever imported food we found at the Tesco down the street. Once, someone brought a pizza from the new pizzeria next to Baskin-Robbins down on Shi Yu Wei Lu, and everyone commented on how much they missed cheese and tomato sauce and bread.

Eventually, we moved beyond our apartments and out into the city. We often met at Sophie's World, a dark, laid-back pub near Govern-ment Square, in the center of the city. It was a good place to meet other foreigners. It had a long bar and a few scattered tables and cold(ish) beer. Sometimes we'd play a popular drinking game called Liar's Dice, where we took turns bidding and calling each other out as liars. Most of the time though we just talked about China—the strange fashions, the noisy traffic, the unusual English names some of our students chose (Junky, Close, Narcissus)—until we got bored and wandered down to a nearby nightclub.

"I can't get anyone's attention," Lynda said once while we were drinking at Sophie's. "Chinese men are too timid to even talk to me and foreign men are only interested in Chinese women. I feel like I'm invisible."

This feeling of invisibility was something Lynda noticed right away. During one of the parties our first month in China, Dan told us about an American who had a Chinese wife, and Lynda, without even trying to sound spiteful, spat out, "Who doesn't" in a dry monotone. We laughed because it was delivered at just the right moment, with just the right amount of cynicism and dryness, and because we wondered whether there was some truth to what was implied with Lynda's statement— that some men came to China looking for Chinese wives. Later, we impersonated Lynda by drawing out the *o* and snapping the second word like a whip. We brought imaginary cigarettes to our lips, took long, slow drags, and in deep, husky rasps said *Whooooo doesn't* before flamboyantly flipping the cigarettes away from our mouths. I named this impersonation *Plynda* and constructed a backstory where she was a late-night radio show host who chain-smoked cigarettes while chatting with truckers and prostitutes and lonely housewives live on-air. *Who doesn't* was her catchphrase, her calling card, her rebel yell.

"You should just walk up to men and start talking," I often replied when Lynda started talking about men.

When I'd say this, Lynda would just look at me sideways and say, "I'm too old-fashioned for that."

Lynda *was* old-fashioned in a lot of ways. During the year we taught in China together, she never told me her age. Once, I asked and she smiled slyly and said, "A lady never reveals her age."

I didn't fully understand Lynda's frustrations with being invisible in China. Part of this was because I was young and somewhat carefree and didn't feel as if I needed to settle down yet. Often, I felt the opposite of invisible in China; I couldn't get people to stop watching me. When I went shopping at Tesco, people would often stop and stare at me while I placed something in my cart. If they were particularly bold, they would lean their torso over and peer into my cart just to see what I was buying. At bars and restaurants and just walking down the street outside the university, I felt noticed, seen. Everyone knew I was there. It wasn't so much that I could feel their eyes on me as I made my way around China but rather that I could feel this energy and curiosity and animosity all at once. And part of me loved it. There was something thrilling about all that attention.

~

I was in the foreign faculty's shared office space when I heard that Lynda had spent several hours overnight being questioned by Chinese police. The story of the night came out in fragments. Someone had stolen Lynda's purse while she waited for a taxi outside Sophie's. The purse contained her phone and wallet, and without them, she had no way to call for help. So, she just started walking toward her apartment.

Later, Lynda told me other things about that night, but the morning after I heard what had happened, I just stared at her empty desk in our shared office space and felt guilty because I should have been there, to call the police, to pay for the taxi, to make sure she got home. Being the oldest of six, I had this instinct to play the "big brother," and the more I heard about Lynda's night, the guiltier I felt about staying home that night and watching pirated episodes of *Heroes* instead of joining her at Sophie's.

Around this time, I had taken to standing in the enclosed patio off the living room of my fifth-floor apartment, looking out at the community around me and thinking about my neighbors. I lived in one of eight nearly identical apartment buildings just north of the university. From my patio, I could see the people coming and going through the front gate. Some would mill around the driveway and courtyard between the buildings. Others would rush between the buildings. I liked to watch the shop owners close their little stores on the first floor and saunter off to their apartments. Sometimes I'd see people talking on cell phones in the courtyard and I'd make up the little conversations they were having. Other times I'd look into the windows of the building across the driveway from mine and see other people in their apartments, sitting on couches and moving about their rooms, and I'd imagine what their lives were like. I imagined what it would be like to really be a part of this community, not just some temporary foreigner looking on from the fringes. I still liked some of the attention being a novelty had given me, but that feeling had started to fade, and I was wondering when I'd start to feel like more than just this oddity in China. I didn't realize then that it takes a while to feel fully integrated into a new environment. Hemingway spent his entire life searching for that feeling.

After hearing about Lynda's night, I looked at my neighbors in a different way. I found myself watching them and picturing secret, *sinister* lives. I had become suspicious of my surroundings, and I wasn't sure how to feel about this. I wanted to stay in that naive state of mind I had experienced when I first arrived in China, the one where I saw only beauty and wonder and novelty. I didn't want to imagine the darker parts I had pretended to ignore as a clueless foreigner. But part of adapting to your surroundings, I believed, meant being critical of your surroundings. This meant not looking away from the less than desirable parts. This meant accepting these parts along with the parts I still found beautiful and wondrous. This meant letting my mind be critical of the people I saw in the courtyards and inside apartments and along the street near campus. This meant staring back at them with the same critical eye they used to stare at me.

∼

After fall semester, Lynda flew home to Vermont, while Heather and I took a train south through China, stopping in Xi'an to see the terracotta soldiers and eventually crossing into Vietnam. We spent two months backpacking around Southeast Asia, trying not to think about China but instead being absorbed by our surroundings—the French architecture of Hanoi's Old Quarter; the ancient ruins outside Sukhothai, Thailand; the timid Mekong snaking along the Thailand–Laos border.

One night, while visiting the night market in Luang Prabang, Laos, we met a fortune teller. We had just ordered food at a busy noodle shop, and the only open seats were next to a middle-aged man who appeared to be alone. The man had thin sandy hair, a slender frame, and kind eyes that made you want to confide in him. He introduced himself and asked us about our trip. We told him about taking the train all the way through China, about the week we spent in Vietnam, about flying to Thailand and then gradually making our way north until we caught the slow boat down the Mekong to Luang Prabang. We talked about what we'd seen in Luang Prabang, how we were thinking of renting a motorbike and driving it out into the countryside. He told us about visiting a monastery and watching the monks at sunrise. The man worked as a holistic healer, focusing on meditation and massage therapy and general wellness, and dabbled in fortune telling. He asked whether we wanted our fortunes told.

I don't remember what he said to Heather, but when he got to me, he looked me in the eyes and said, "You are living only for yourself."

I wasn't necessarily surprised by the fortune teller's words, but they stuck with me for the rest of my trip through southeast Asia. Later, back in my apartment in China, I stood in my enclosed patio and thought about what the fortune teller had said, how he had seen me. I had been thinking people saw me as this fun-loving, affable foreigner curious about everything around him. But the fortune teller got me wondering whether I had been wrong about how I was being perceived. *Is that what people thought when they looked at me, this selfish guy living only for himself, someone who couldn't be tied down, who only really cared for himself, who wandered and wandered and never really stayed in one place long enough to make an impact or develop lasting relationships?*

It was night, and instead of trying to look out the windows at my neighbors I looked at my own reflection silhouetted in the glass. I stepped back, and my reflection grew small and thin. I got closer, and my silhouette got wider, fatter, darker. I took my camera out and started taking pictures of my reflection, some crouched down, some with my index and middle fingers in the shape of a V, some of me just standing still. I didn't know what to think of the silhouettes, so I posted them on

Facebook, inviting others to tell me what they saw. I wanted others to tell me they didn't see a selfish man living only for himself. I wanted them to tell me the fortune teller from Luang Prabang was wrong.

No one did.

~

Our version of Hemingway's Closerie des Lilas was a little restaurant near the north gate of the university. It was at the end of a row of restaurants and little shops, along the route I walked from my apartment to my office at the university. We stumbled upon the restaurant one day while we were trying to find someplace to have dinner. A woman stood in the doorway smiling and waving us toward her, saying *laowei, laowei*—literally, "old foreigner." She reminded me of the character Dorothy from *Golden Girls*, with her gray fluff of hair and her Big Bird-like stature. She had a big smile, sparkling eyes, a motherly presence. She spoke to us in rapid Mandarin, and when we replied with the little Mandarin we knew, she didn't frown or tsk-tsk the way the taxi drivers did.

The restaurant quickly became one of my favorite spots. Once the weather turned nice, we met there in the late afternoon after classes. We sat at plastic tables on the patio out front, under umbrellas with Chinese beer logos, drinking and using chopsticks to pluck half-moon pieces of cucumber from a ceramic bowl. We made a point of getting to the restaurant early, before all the noisy students and drunk businessmen invaded the plaza outside the restaurant and made everything loud and annoying.

"How's Lynda these days?" I asked one day near the beginning of spring semester.

It was a beautiful afternoon, sunny and warm. In front of us, two men were setting up the charcoal grill used to make *chuan'r*—grilled meat sticks. Next to the grill was a table with dried red pepper flakes, sesame and cumin seeds, salt flakes, and oil. The men unspooled an extension cord and plugged it into a lamp, which they positioned over the table.

Lynda lounged in a plastic patio chair, smoking and watching the men. She had returned to China numb after the break between semesters.

Her doctor had changed her medication, so instead of the joyful person she was in the fall—before her night in Chinese police custody—she walked around China as if in a daze. We'd go to Sophie's for drinks or Starbucks to grade papers, and she'd stare off into the middle distance, her eyelids half-closed, present but also not. We never talked about her night in Chinese police custody. Instead, we tried to act as if nothing had changed.

"Oh, you know," she said. "Same old China."

I smiled because I wished that were true. I wished the "same old China" she was referring to were the one from last fall, when we first arrived, when everything was new and exciting. But the China Lynda was referring to was one that continually made her frustrated, one she felt invisible in. And while I also saw some of Lynda's frustrations in China, I was still transfixed by the country and people I encountered. I still saw the beauty I saw when I first arrived, but since I'd started to think a little more critically about my surroundings, I started to see China on a new level. I appreciated things I hadn't noticed before, like the old men exercising on equipment in the courtyard outside my apartment and the strange beauty in a crowded train depot lobby late at night. Things I had found annoying when I first arrived felt less so that spring. I liked to think that I was changing, that I had started thinking less about how my surroundings were changing me and more about how I could adapt to my surroundings, like a *true* expatriate would.

We watched the men grilling *chuan'r* for a while, and eventually, we ordered for the whole table. The meat was spicy and smoky and charred crisp around the edges. I took a swig of my beer, plucked a cucumber slice from the bowl, and leaned back in my plastic chair. I liked those nights because we could sit on the patio drinking and eating *chuan'r* and watching the night come alive around us.

Around 7 o'clock the *gonbei*-ing students and businessmen arrived. We stuck around a little longer, but then I said goodbye to Lynda and Heather and started walking slowly down the street toward my apartment complex. It was one of the first warm nights that spring, so the street was noisy. A woman sat with a giant white dog outside the porn shop. The gambling place next door was packed full of men, yelling and yelping at television screens. Just outside the shops, a man spat directly in front of me, not at me but close enough for me to notice. I walked by another man vomiting in the street, a cell phone pressed up against his ear. A pack of young men briskly passed me on their way to the computer cafe down the street. I heard a loud boom and looked up. Directly above my head a couple fireworks exploded into purple and green flowers, the sparks cascading down to the horizon.

I'd gotten used to all these distractions individually in China, but something about all of them together felt new and exciting. *This is how it must feel when everything falls into place around you.*

~

In my second year in China, I made a concerted effort to adapt to my new surroundings. I listened more closely to the other faculty when they told me about their students and their stories. I asked more questions, tried to understand the lives of the people I met in China better. I became less frustrated with everyday annoyances and came to appreciate them as integral to the experience of living in China. I even tried using my limited Mandarin to talk to taxi drivers, something I never did during my first year in China.

I had started to believe that I'd found the expatriate life I'd read about in *A Moveable Feast.*

Then, in the spring of my second year, my father had a mild stroke back in North Dakota. I talked to my mother through Skype from my apartment in China. She was at the hospital. My four brothers and my sister were with her. At one point my mother started crying and had to hand the phone to my oldest brother, Brandon. *He's going to be fine,* my brother said, but his words didn't give me much relief.

After the call, I sat in my apartment and stared at the wall. I hated not being there. I wanted to be there to comfort them and talk to my father and reassure him that everything would be all right. I was the oldest of my siblings, so it felt like my responsibility to comfort everyone in times like this. I hated that I was so far away—so far removed from everyone else—and that I was the only one not there. I felt untethered, disconnected. My quest to find Hemingway's expat life had separated me from the people I loved. I thought that if I kept wandering and living only for myself—as I'd been doing for two years—all my relationships would erode. It was a little extreme, but my father's stroke helped me realize how selfishly I'd been living, how the man from Luang Prabang was right. There was a part of me—the part I'd been ignoring—urging me to think about someone other than myself. And for once I listened to that part.

I declined an offer to teach in China another year and returned to North Dakota.

~

When we were in China together, I gave Lynda a notebook I'd found at a shop on campus, with space to record new words and phrases. It was designed to help someone learn a new language, and I had filled it with words and phrases our friend group had used in China, the little language we had created together. There was *bippy*, the word we used for the bizarre fashion choices we saw in China, and *split pants*, trousers for toddlers with slits in the crotch since diapers were expensive in China, and *zhège* and *nàge* (*this one* and *that one*), common among foreigners like us who didn't know much of the language and resorted to a lot of pointing.

But the first entry in the dictionary was *who doesn't*.

Who doesn't took on multiple meanings during our time in China. We used it as a noun to refer to a foreign man who was looking for a Chinese wife or any foreigner who seemed more interested in hooking up. We used it for shared frustrations or as an expression of boredom when we sat around our apartments lamenting about home. One of us would say how much we missed some aspect of home, and the others would take drags from imaginary cigarettes and say *who doesn't* in raspy whispers. In this way, *who doesn't* became more than just a commentary on expatriate emptiness and foreign men hooking up with Chinese women. I came to see it as our version of the oysters from Hemingway's *A Moveable Feast*. For me, the phrase came to represent this feeling so many expatriates experience, how we venture into unfamiliar territory in search of meaning and community, unsure of what we'll find. How, for some of us, that feeling never goes away.

~

I got a job at a tribal college ninety miles north of my hometown. I lived fourteen miles from the Canadian border, in an apartment across from Walmart at the edge of town. Beyond the Walmart were prairie fields with tall grasses all the way to the horizon. I'd sit on my balcony watching these grasses, thinking about the farm I grew up on and how tranquil it all made me feel. Eventually, I came to appreciate the stillness of North Dakota after so many years away. In the mornings, I'd drive east to work at the college. Most days, I struggled to get through to my students. Many of them lived on or near the reservation and had distractions beyond the classroom. On the weekends, I would visit my parents and help with their hardware store. I liked being back near them. I felt needed. I felt closer to them than ever before. If something happened again, I wouldn't be on the other side of the world.

This new routine worked for a little while, but then I'd return alone to my apartment across from Walmart and my mind would wander off to China and other places I could be. After our year in China together, Lynda returned to Vermont, where she felt bored and restless while she waited for another opportunity. We emailed regularly. She told me about her lazy students, the leather coat she bought from a Russian woman, her trip to Montreal. She told me about not dating, how she'd occasionally get hit on by men—a party where someone said "oh-la-la" about her, a Dunkin' Donuts employee who flirted with her. When her graduate school friend published an essay about finding a husband and having a baby, she sent me a link and lamented how lonely she was in Vermont. More than once she commented on how she felt her life was on hold until something better came along. She eventually took a job teaching in Shanghai and moved to China again. She periodically emailed me updates about her new life abroad. I came to look forward to these emails because they reminded me how exciting the life of an expatriate could be. I wanted to live vicariously through her attempts to find her way back into China, and with each email from Lynda I felt wanderlust trying to pull me away, trying to get me to go exploring again.

Six months after moving to Shanghai, Lynda emailed to say that she'd abruptly left her job in the middle of her contract and flown home because she felt lonelier than ever before. Her next email came six months after she moved to Tucson "for her last chance at a rewarding life." I got a few emails from her while she was in Tucson, but then, after five years of emailing back and forth, an email to her bounced back undelivered. Her account had been deleted. I waited because I figured she'd eventually email, apologizing and explaining that she had to delete her old email account because she was hacked or because of her malfunctioning computer. But she never did. I emailed again, to two different email accounts, but all my emails bounced back. I checked Facebook. I checked the directory of the college she used to work for. I Googled her name, hoping not to find an obituary, but found only a smattering of old publications and a listing on RateMyProfessor.com. I contacted our mutual friend Dan and asked if he'd heard from her. He hadn't talked to Lynda in a few years. I waited. Two months of no contact eventually turned into five years, and I realized that maybe I wasn't the kind of friend to Lynda I thought I was. Maybe, in the end, I was just another distraction.

In the years since I last heard from Lynda, I've often thought about a line from *A Moveable Feast* where Hemingway comments on the memory of his time in Paris: "We always returned to it no matter who we were or how it was changed or with what difficulties, or ease, it could be reached. Paris was always worth it and you received return for whatever you brought to it." I kept going back to my first few months in China when I was just trying to figure things out and wondering whether going to China had been worth it. Then I remember that Hemingway left Paris vowing never again to live in a city. He moved from place to place—Key West, Wyoming, Cuba, Idaho. He never stayed in one place for very long. He kept looking and looking, trying to fill that emptiness, the way Lynda did, the way so many of us do.

You Think I'm a Boy

She was always a little bit of a mystery, my student named Shiny. Then and now. She sat in front of all my classes the first year I taught in China, but now, ten years later, I have a hard time fully describing her. Like many of the students—both men and women—she had dark hair, cut short, that framed her face. She had small, wire-rimmed glasses over dark, steely eyes, this stone-cold look about her, one I often found difficult to read. She wasn't alone in this regard. I found many of my students' expressions difficult to read.

There was more. What am I missing?

She was bright and knew the answers to the questions I asked, but she wasn't overly curious. She didn't raise her hand to ask questions during class as David or Julie often did. Nor did she chat with me about America and traveling the way Isabella and Cheese liked to after class. She didn't do anything extraordinary to make herself stand out from her fellow students. She was pleasant and quiet and smart. I saw all of that.

But she is memorable to me now because of what I *didn't* see.

Near the end of my first year teaching English composition at a university in Shenyang, Shiny came into my empty classroom and sat before me, in the chair I'd placed across from my own, but I didn't really see her. I wish I had. I was homesick and lonely and frustrated with my own inability to adapt in China, and my mind kept drifting off to my upcoming vacation to Shanghai and my flight home that summer. We talked about her plans. She asked for a letter of recommendation for graduate school, which I said I'd gladly write. Then, without missing a beat, she looked me in the eyes, stone-faced and serious as she always was when interacting with me, and said, "I think you think I'm a boy."

I bowed my head. I couldn't look her in the eyes because I knew she knew she was right. She was my student for an entire academic year—two back-to-back, fifteen-week semesters—and that entire time I thought she was a young man.

~

I lived alone in a two-bedroom apartment on the fifth floor of a large concrete building just north of campus, one of eight nearly identical apartment buildings, all painted a dusty shade of peach. In the mornings, I walked from my apartment to campus and marveled at all the activity along the way. Old men sipping porridge from ceramic bowls. Women lifting fried dough sticks out of vats of sizzling oil. Teens walking to class with steamed buns in their hands. In the evenings, I passed a bathhouse with puddles of vomit splattered on the pavement near the door, a sex shop with a shaggy dog sitting on the stoop, a cyber café filled with college students playing video games. Inside my apartment, I watched pirated movies or read or graded my students' papers. I kept one of the bedroom doors closed because a patch of mold grew in one corner, and I didn't know whom to talk to to make it go away. In the other bedroom, someone had taped pictures of shirtless Asian heartthrobs inside the armoire, so every morning when I got dressed, I was greeted by a smattering of hunks with hairless chests and perfectly wind-blown hair. One night I got drunk on cheap beer and gave catchphrases to the cherubs frosted onto my balcony doors. I cut out dialogue bubbles from Post-it notes and pasted them above the cherubs' heads. *I once killed a man in Reno*, one said. *I'm a perky brunette on the skids!* another exclaimed.

A few weeks into living in China, I bought a durian fruit from an outdoor market down the street from my apartment, and I decided to give it to my friend Lynda for her birthday. The owner of the fruit stand gave me the durian in a plastic bag. It wasn't terribly heavy, probably six or seven pounds, but it was awkward, and I had to walk several blocks back to my apartment with the barbs of the fruit tearing apart the bag. I stopped a lot, to rest or switch arms, and the entire time I was carrying the fruit, I thought how oddly exciting it was to be carrying a durian fruit through the streets of a Chinese city. *Look at me. I have a durian. And it's ripping apart this bag,* I thought, looking around to see if anyone had noticed me.

I often stopped for *jianbing* (eggy pancakes) at one of the food carts lining the street near my apartment. The cart was owned by a friendly, middle-aged couple who smiled widely every time I stepped up to their cart. At first, they asked me questions, trying to get me to talk to them about my life, but when they realized I didn't know much Mandarin, they gave up. They just handed me my food and smiled.

When I tried speaking Mandarin in those first few months, people chuckled or scoffed at my poor pronunciation. Shopkeepers. Taxi drivers. Chinese tourists I met downtown. They all looked at me like I was this little boy still learning what to say and how to act, still getting used to his surroundings. I learned to stay quiet, to spit back the few phrases I'd memorized, to let them think of me as a child.

∼

The summer before I left home for China, Beijing hosted the XXIX Olympiad. I watched the opening ceremonies in Fargo with my brother Brandon and his wife. I was preparing myself mentally for leaving for China, and so much about the country was uncertain to me, so I watched the ceremony with the same curiosity and wonder I had as a child.

When I was a boy, I loved watching the Olympic Games. My family and I would gather around the television to watch athletes from all around the world jump and run and swim and do all sorts of things. I especially liked the opening ceremony, where the athletes marched into the stadium in groups. After the announcer would say the name of the country, I'd repeat it, slowly, quietly, and wonder what it was like to live in such a place. *Zimbabwe. Romania. Brazil.* I never thought I'd visit those countries, so I watched and wondered and built worlds inside my head. I imagined lands so bizarre, so different, so alive that there was no way these imagined places were real.

∼

I traced my mistake with Shiny back to the first day of class, when the administration handed me a roster of my students with several columns of information. I remember skimming the columns with Chinese names, pinyin family names, and pinyin given names, thinking I'd use the students' pinyin given names once I got to know them a little better. But on that first day, I focused on the column with the English names.

All students were required to adopt an English name. Sometimes students are given names by their oral English instructors, but most of the time students choose their own names, often from magazines or movies or television. I remember a male student named Juno and another one named Archer. I remember a Felicity and an Avril. I know I had a Phoebe and a Monica, but I don't remember if there was a Rachel as well. I certainly didn't have a Chandler or a Ross.

There were also the unusual and "mistake" names I assumed were given to students by cruel foreign faculty as a joke or were mistakenly copied from other sources. Cheese. Purple. Blender. One of my students was named D. B. Copper. When I asked him if he meant D. B. Cooper, he shook his head and repeated his name. Those were the only English words I ever heard him say. Even worse off was a student named Nudy. She was a shy girl, with big eyes and a sad face. She sat in the front row of every class, and because she had a "mistake name," I remember her more vividly now than I do many of her classmates. I didn't have the heart to tell her that the foreign faculty laughed every time they heard her name.

I do remember a narrow column next to the English names—filled with Fs and Ms—that I skipped over entirely because I didn't think it was necessary, a column with information that could have prevented Shiny from sitting down before me and saying, "I think you think I'm a boy."

Gender.

~

I knew I shouldn't have played favorites, but I liked the women in my classes better than the men. The women were the curious ones. They asked questions. They were interested in art and music and traveling.

Most important, they weren't afraid to talk to me about their lives. The men just seemed interested in basketball. I'm exaggerating a bit, but the women just seemed more alert and alive. Also, sadder? More hopeful? More real? I don't know. I could be projecting this onto them.

Many of my students wrote about the typical stuff I'd heard about Chinese people—the loneliness that comes with being an only child, the pressure to succeed in school, the fear of failure in a growing society—but the stories I heard from some of the women tapped into the insecurities and fears I'd imagined many of them had. Tiffany—a large-headed girl who sat in the front row and made disruptive, yet charming, comments during most classes—wrote about a childhood fear of dogs that manifested in drawings in her notebooks and in the margins of her essays. It was unexpected from her because she was the class clown, the one everyone relied on to say something strange or humorous during class. Jane—a quiet girl who rarely spoke up in class—wrote about her distant father, a businessman who, from the way she described him, was nearly absent from her life. Faye sat in the back of most classes but always appeared alert and interested during my lectures. She wrote about the desire to travel abroad with a kind of sad hopefulness that comes from the realization that it may never happen.

I learned so much about my students from their writing. The more I got to know them, the more I started to think about the possibilities that were ahead of them. They were motivated. They were dedicated. They worked together, valued loyalty, and expected the best from one another. Many dreamed of getting a good job. For the ones that shined most brightly in my mind—Tiffany and Jane and Faye—I created imagined futures. I imagined Jane running her own business, something that also allowed her time to spend with her family. Faye was a dreamer, so I pictured her painting on the banks of a foreign river, somewhere with history and charm. In my mind, Tiffany created radio advertisements or worked on a sitcom, something where her zaniness would be appreciated. I empathized with their desire to be seen and understood. I wanted to be seen and understood as well.

∼

On weekends, I drank with the other foreign faculty, the ones who'd been in China for a while, and they told me stories about China's obsession with success. Many of the stories were related to the "one-child" policy, which created a culture where male children were valued more than females. *The culture is obsessed with men,* the faculty said, and they told me stories created by the policy. Chinese businessmen cheating on their wives if they had female children in order to get a male heir. Baby girls being abandoned in fields or shopping centers or down dark alleys. Sons turning into "little emperors," spoiled and cherished because of their gender.

I couldn't really understand what it felt like to be a woman in China, but I could have paid attention to what the women in my class were telling me during and after class and in their writing. I could have listened more closely to what they had to say instead of thinking about how I could correct their grammar. I could have written messages of support in the margins of their essays, encouraging them to be honest and truthful and to use their voice. When they stopped me after class to ask questions about my personal life or just to practice their English, I could have been more patient and understanding instead of rushing the awkward little conversations along.

∼

Written Mandarin used to have one gender-neutral pronoun—他— for "he," "she," and "it." But, in 1920, the Chinese linguist and poet Liu Bannong proposed adding a new character—她—for "she." This new character was met with a lot of opposition. One opponent claimed that the new character was phonetically inferior to another pronoun—*yi*. Supporters of the feminist movement rejected the new character because they felt that it could create further separation between the rights of men and women in China. The biggest opposition to the new character came from those who felt it was a product of Western influence and felt that adopting a new character was groveling to the West. Ultimately, Lui Bannong's song 教我如何不想她 (*Tell Me How to Stop Thinking of Her*) increased the popularity of the new character and helped it become adopted into the Mandarin language.

∼

"Maybe she wanted you to think she was a boy," my friend Diana said after I told her about Shiny.

She could have. Or she wanted to be seen as nonbinary.

I knew very little then about nonbinary gender identities, in China or elsewhere. I didn't know where on the spectrum of gender identities Shiny placed herself, whether she identified as having two or more genders, whether she moved between genders or considered herself other-gendered. Or whether she even saw herself on the spectrum. I didn't know what it felt like to live outside the gender binary, to not define your gender identity and not really care whether people understood this decision. And I didn't know what it felt like to feel this way in China, whether the culture was more or less accepting of nonbinary gender identities than America's, or whether China's one-child policy and glorification of male children created added pressure for females to appear male.

I knew very little about Shiny, I realized, and after she said, "I think you think I'm a boy," I wasn't sure whether it was even acceptable or appropriate to ask how she identified.

I wish I had had the courage to ask.

I only knew what I saw, and what I saw was a bright young man.

$\sim$

The administration at the business college where I taught gave foreign faculty gifts all academic year. In the fall, they gave us boxes of apples. The apples were mealy little knobs with no flavor, so I gave most of them to my students. For the Dragon Boat Festival, they gave us thirty salted duck eggs, each individually wrapped and laid out side by side in a Styrofoam box. I didn't eat any of those, choosing instead to give them to my students in exchange for answers in class.

In the spring, they gave us mini bicycles. The wheels were the size of dinner plates, but the seats and handlebars raised up to accommodate teens and young adults. I rode mine around the square outside the business building, laughing while trying to do wheelies.

Later, I walked my bike to the north gate, then hopped on and rode it up and down the street a couple of times. My knees raised up and tapped my chest, so I had to alternate between standing and fiercely pushing down on the pedals and resting back on the seat. It was warm and there was a slight breeze, and while I pedaled, I ignored the people stopping to watch me ride by, the shopkeepers and students and rickshaw drivers staring at this ridiculous *laowai* riding such a small bicycle. I just pedaled and laughed and spun around the corners and didn't care whether they saw me as a boy. The longer I spent in China, the less I seemed to care what people thought of me.

~

I could have spent more time learning the language, but I found Mandarin to be difficult and I made up excuses for why the language wasn't sinking in. *I don't have the ear for Mandarin,* I'd say. *My tongue gets twisted shifting between all the different tones.* Or I'd repeat a statistic I'd read online—*China has the largest number of English-language learners in the world*—to justify not learning more.

During a Mandarin lesson before arriving in China, an instructor used the pinyin word *ma* to describe the four Mandarin tones. She wrote four *mas* on the chalkboard, each one with a different symbol above the *a*. *Ma* can have different meanings depending on which tone is used, she explained. First tone *ma* means "mother." Third tone *ma* means "horse." In my notes of this lesson, I have question marks over the other two *mas*; I don't think she ever told us what those *mas* meant. She then described how the meaning of a Mandarin sentence can change depending on which tone is used. This prompted the leader of the program to make a joke about calling your mother a horse. Or calling a horse your mother. I forget which.

I have notes on other words learned during that lesson—*ni hao* (hello), *yi dian* (very little), *Ken Da Ji* (Kentucky Fried Chicken). During my first year in China, I used many of those words, but I never really understood what I was saying. I could *hear* the different tones, but when it came to speaking to them, my tongue got all twisted and knotted up. *Ma.* Did I say "horse" or "mother"? I wasn't sure. Instead of learning the tones, I listened for how things were said, memorized them, and spat them back out when needed. I learned to count to ten this way, by listening to the shopkeepers say the numbers when they gave me my change. I learned the words for "steamed bun" (*bao zi*), "that" (*na ge*), and "beer" (*pi jiu*). Often, I would get asked where I was from, and at first, I would only stare back silently. Eventually I learned the word *meiguoren*—American—and I would spit that out, sometime as an answer to questions other than "Where are you from?"

I tried to learn more. In my third week in China, I started attending Mandarin language classes at the International Education School. They were taught by young Chinese women and attended by international students from Japan, Iran, and Kyrgyzstan. I was nervous about attending the classes because I knew so little of the Mandarin language. I found it was easiest to think of myself as a schoolchild again, to let go of everything and try to soak in as much as possible.

During one of my first lessons, I was asked to approach the chalkboard and write the vowels associated with different pinyin "finals." We were learning the different vowel sounds, and I felt pretty good about the *u* I had written on the board. But, when I got back to my seat, the instructor shook her head, picked up the chalk, and circled the *u* I had written.

"What's wrong with this?" she said in English.

I didn't know. I looked at it again. It looked like the *us* I had written my entire life, an upward swoop, the right side bulging out farther than it should. I looked at the instructor. The only explanation I could think of was that it wasn't the correct answer; I had written the wrong vowel sound.

The instructor looked around the classroom for an answer from someone else. Then, finding no answers among us, she stepped to the board and drew the tail on the end of my *u*. I had forgotten to come down from my swoop, to create the tail. I hadn't drawn the tail on my *us* since elementary school.

I was frustrated with myself, so I looked down at my hands and felt the same small shame I had felt in school when I'd answered a question wrong. *How could I look at something for so long and not see what I was supposed to see?* That *u* was definitely a *u*, but there was something more I wasn't seeing. I wasn't paying attention to the details, to the little things like the tails of the *us*.

I never returned to class after that.

⌇

Maybe, I just wasn't a very observant teacher. If I follow this line of thinking, I can pinpoint another place where my thinking about Shiny was off.

Near the end of the second semester, eight months after I arrived in China, we were working on a writing activity in which students had to share their writing with a partner. Shiny had partnered up with David, another excellent student. While I was walking around the classroom, David raised his hand. I stepped over next to his desk. He asked me a question in which he referred to Shiny. I don't remember what the question was, but I do remember David using "she" to refer to Shiny. Hearing this, I thought, *Shiny is a boy.* But then I remembered that many of the students had language problems of their own. Many of them struggled with differentiating between "he" and "she" in English. This was common because in spoken Mandarin "he," "she," and "it" all sound the same. In written Mandarin, there are three different characters—他 (he), 她 (she), and 它 (it)—but when spoken, these three characters sound identical—*tā*. Instead of having different tones for each character (like *ma*), *tā* has one tone (the high level, first tone) for all three.

Many of my fellow instructors commented on how students would often call each other the wrong gender during class. Some of the students would catch themselves midsentence, laugh awkwardly, and correct their pronouns. Most often, instructors would choose to either correct the pronoun for the student or let the mistake slide. Thinking I was being a good teacher, I attempted to use David's mistake as a teaching moment.

"She?" I said.

Both David and Shiny looked at me oddly, and I instantly knew something was wrong.

⌇

Recently, there's been a push to go back to one gender-neutral option for referring to someone in written Mandarin. Some argue for using 你 (you) or 他们 (them) or going back to using 他 (he).Others suggest using the pinyin *tā* in the place of 他 and 她, two letters surrounded by lines of Chinese characters.

I like to think I learned a lot from my mistake with Shiny. I am more careful about making assumptions. I spend more time listening and less time talking. I ask my students for their pronouns and do activities to encourage an inclusive classroom. I remain open and curious about their lives, and when I don't understand, I ask questions.

Sometimes, I feel like I'm doing enough. Most of the time, I feel like I could do more.

∼

After Shiny said, "I think you think I'm a boy," I should have admitted my mistake. I should have swallowed my pride, leaned forward, and apologized. Maybe then, Shiny would have let down her own guard, talked to me as if I were a friend or mentor, and explained her own fears about living in China. In this version of the story, we might have hugged or shaken hands or smiled at each other before going our separate ways.

But I didn't do any of that. I was embarrassed and afraid to admit that I was wrong, that I could overlook something—someone!—even when the person was right in front of me. I feared Shiny would look at me the same way the taxi drivers and food vendors and others who tried to talk to me in China did, with this mix of wonder and pity. When she said, "I think you think I'm a boy," she seemed to be saying, *Why don't you see me?*, and I didn't have a good answer for that. So, like a child, I lied and looked away.

"No," I said back to Shiny, weakly, unable to look her in the eyes. "I don't think you're a boy."

Shiny may have presented herself as nonbinary, but because of everything I didn't know about being nonbinary and the influence of language and politics on gender identity in China, I saw her only as male. And that isn't her fault. It's mine.

I tried to present myself as a confident, self-assured young man while living in China, but, inside, I felt very much like a boy, a boy who liked to ride his little bike around the neighborhood and answer every question asked in Mandarin with *meiguoren*. Thinking about Shiny and how we present ourselves to the world, I wonder how much of that boy other people saw while I lived there. Thinking about it now, I wonder if they saw anything *other than* a boy, a child who had so much to learn.

Shiny and I both left China after that. She left to study at a university in Missouri, and I went home for a month that summer. But I returned that September, for one more year of teaching, hoping I wouldn't make the same mistakes I had my first year.

A few years later, I came across pictures of Shiny on Facebook. One was taken at a birthday party where she was standing in the back row of a group of friends. Another was a professional headshot, same short haircut, same wire-framed glasses, same tight-lipped smile, but she was wearing a black blazer, a blue button-down shirt, and a patterned tie cinched up to her neck. When I looked at the photos, I didn't see the same student I'd taught in China. She seemed more self-assured, so much more prepared to handle the world around her than I was while in China, and seeing Shiny growing confident in her own gender identity made me very happy.

A Sailor's Life

When I got to the waiting area outside the gate at Beijing Capital International Airport—completely out of breath and slightly disheveled from running through several terminals—it was empty and still as I'd never seen before. Not a single person sat in the plastic seats. People weren't crowded around the ticket counter. The glass door to the jetway was closed, and beyond it I could see an empty bridge. Above the counter the display still had the number and time for my flight to Kunming, and below that two women were busily typing into computers, ignoring the breathless foreigner staring at them from across the empty waiting area, the one who'd just missed his flight.

I dropped my backpack at my feet, bent over, and placed my hands on my knees. I shouldn't have been late. I'd carefully calculated the time it would take me to get from my hotel to the airport—the metro train, the ticket counter, the security checkpoint. What I hadn't anticipated was how hard it would be to say goodbye to a man I'd known for only a few months. At the edge of that airport waiting area, I took a few deep breaths and then quietly cursed myself for looping my arms around the man's waist, for pulling him tightly into me and thinking that I could hold onto him forever.

I grabbed my backpack by the strap and slowly walked to the ticket counter.

"The plane door is closed, sir," the attendant said without looking at me.

I didn't say anything back, only nodded. I could still see the plane at the end of the jetway. It was surrounded by the sky of a Chinese morning—murky and omniscient and gray. I wasn't sure what else to do, so I just blinked back at the woman and waited. I watched as she typed something into her computer. She told me that there was another flight to Kunming, leaving an hour later, and directed me to a different counter to buy another ticket.

I could have gone to Japan with the Joes, two friends I'd been teaching with. I had considered it because it is so much easier traveling in a foreign country when you have someone else to lean on. Plus, I enjoyed their company and had traveled with them multiple times. We'd drank in bars in the Sunlitun district in Beijing and had hiked sections of the Great Wall and had seen the Buddhist statues carved into the cliffs of the Longman Caves. But I wanted to wander around China alone. After two years living in China, I'd built up enough skills to finally venture out on my own, and I wanted to prove to myself that I'd acquired enough knowledge about the people and the culture and the land to move through the country easily. I had to have something to show for two years of living there and had designed a trip to test myself on what I'd learned. The plan was to spend a few days in Beijing visiting a man I'd met a few months earlier—to see if there was anything between us worth holding onto—and then fly to Kunming to start a ten-day solo backpacking trip across Yunnan Province, in the southwestern corner of China, visiting Dali and Lijiang and culminating in hiking the Tiger Leaping Gorge, a 12,434-foot-deep canyon, one of the deepest in the world.

I was normally so organized and prepared when it came to traveling. I had never before missed a flight, never even had to run to catch a flight before. But something about this man and the few days I spent in Beijing with him had thrown me off, messed with my normally organized self. I started to doubt my ability to travel through China alone. As I walked to the new waiting area, I felt this deep sense of dread sink into my stomach and wondered whether missing my flight was an omen of what was to come. I was still an awkward foreigner in a strange land, still an expat exaggerating his abilities to adapt, still an outsider easily distracted by beauty and glittering novelty.

Even if I wanted to believe otherwise.

~

The first book with a major queer character that I remember reading was *Giovanni's Room* by James Baldwin. I checked it out from my college's library and read it in my bedroom one afternoon. I was twenty-two, dating my second boyfriend, and still very much confused about who I was supposed to be. I don't remember why I'd sought out the book or where I'd heard about it, but I remember the feelings of shame and excitement that reading about two men falling in love in a tiny room on the outskirts of Paris stirred. When I got to the part where David explains how Giovanni had awakened "an itch" he could no longer stop scratching, I had to put the book down and stare out my bedroom window for a while because it all felt too real and raw to me. I was just beginning to feel my own itch, and reading about David's struggles with both hating Giovanni for awakening that itch and loving him just as fiercely made me nervous and afraid for my own future as a gay man.

Certain moments from *Giovanni's Room* stuck with me—David and Giovanni sharing a kilo of cherries on the street, Jacques advising David to "love him and let him love you," David leaving the room for the last time. But the scene I thought about most in the years after reading the novel came near the end of the first part of the book. David is in southern France, having left Giovanni and Paris, and the caretaker of the house he is staying in stops by to check on him. The caretaker is an old Italian woman, and while she is inventorying the house, she utters a few lines I still think about because they get to the heart of my own wandering soul: "But you do not have the intention of just wandering through the world like a sailor? I am sure that would make your mother very unhappy. You will make a home someday?"

At twenty-two, I was just starting to realize that maybe getting married and settling down and building a home with someone wasn't possible for me, even though this was the type of life I'd been conditioned to see as normal when I was growing up. Also, I had yet to meet a happy queer couple, so I wasn't even sure I wanted to commit myself to one person. Maybe there was something else, a different way of being. Maybe I could live this life of a wandering sailor disconnected from the people around him and free to follow his every whim and desire. Maybe that was the life I wanted to live.

After graduate school, I tried out this sailor's life. I took a job teaching in northeast China, and after a year, I moved to another city in China, to take a different teaching job, unworried about what I had left behind. I didn't let a job or friends or my family hold me back. For years, I chased my own internal wanderlust, letting it show me more and more of the world around me and the possibilities of living a different kind of life. It was freeing. I was unburdened by a partner or children or property. I lived only for myself.

Still, there was a part of me hoping something would come along, pin me down, and hold me in place. It was a small part of me, a part I kept buried because I was so used to ignoring my desires. But it was there. I kept it pushed to the back of my mind and only occasionally entertained it.

This desire for someone to snag me by the collar and love me the way Giovanni loved David in that room.

∼

I first met Sen in the spring. I'd come to Beijing with the Joes, but they had dropped me off at a gay club near the Workers' Stadium and gone off to find their own place to drink. For the first hour, I stood near the back of one of the rooms off the main dance floor and threw back a few beers to calm my nervousness. I watched the men around me. My Mandarin was horrible, so instead of approaching anyone I waited for men to come to me. The first guy I met caught my eye while I was looking around. He walked over and leaned in to introduce himself. We chatted for a while about why I was in China and what he liked and didn't like about living there, but eventually he got bored and walked away. That was when I met Sen.

For a while after meeting, we just chatted about China. In between sips from my beer, I asked him where he was from and what he did in China. He replied in brief English phrases, admitting that his English was "bad," but he knew enough to have a conversation. When I ran out of things to say, I asked him whether he wanted to dance, and when he nodded, I grabbed his hand and led him through the crowd to the dance floor. After a few songs of dancing awkwardly near each other, I gently placed my hand on Sen's waist. He stepped closer, took off his glasses, and slid one temple into my collar so his glasses hung from my shirt. He placed his hands on my shoulders and we danced in our own little orbit for a while. When we got tired of dancing, we went up to the second floor where there were couches and soft lighting and found a spot where it wasn't so crowded. Sen had his back against the wall, and I stood before him, one arm up against the wall, the other on his waist. I smiled and he smiled back. Then I leaned in and kissed him. When I leaned my head away, Sen opened his eyes, looked up at me, and said, "I want to be your boyfriend."

After the club, we exchanged usernames for QQ, the messaging app popular in China. Sen sent me messages every day. Most days we'd meet on QQ at the same time and send messages back and forth. Occasionally, we video chatted. I had a horrible habit of biting my nails, and he would tease me when he caught me biting off a hangnail. We chatted about how we spent our days, our pasts, our parents. Slowly, I started to learn more and more about Sen, and gradually I let him know a little about me as well.

During this time, I'd often eat dinner in the faculty dining room at the university I worked at. After dinner I'd take long, melancholy walks around campus. Sometimes one or both of the Joes walked with me. Other times I walked with my colleague Mark. I enjoyed Mark's company, liked hearing his thoughts about teaching and China. The rumor was that Mark's partner had died suddenly and the reason he was in China was because he couldn't stand being in his house back in the U.S. alone. When it was just the two of us out walking, there'd be these long pauses where I'd almost ask him about his partner but then decide against it at the last minute. I didn't want to bring up anything that would make him sad or upset. Instead, I would imagine Mark and his partner in their house together, making dinner, tending to their garden, reading side by side before bed. All these happy domestic scenes of a life lived with someone else, except with two men.

Even though we'd known each other for only a few months, I felt something very real when I was talking with Sen, and I knew I'd regret it if I didn't explore it further. So, when my teaching duties were done and grades were submitted that summer, I decided to fly to Beijing to spend a few days with him before embarking on my solo trip across Yunnan Province. We met at the Beijing Train Station and took the subway to a hotel Sen had found for us. When we got into the room, he took off his backpack and removed a couple bottles of orange juice, several cans of beer, and shrimp-flavored potato chips. Then, he held out a pink envelope in a clear plastic sleeve.

"For you," he said.

I took the envelope and slid it from the sleeve. On the back flap, Sen had written "To byte finger man." I smiled. I knew of his love for computers, so it seemed fitting that he used *byte* instead of *bite*. I opened the flap and removed a greeting card. On the front were two branches, a butterfly, and the words "Best Wishes For You." Inside, Sen had written the following: "My dear: Though my English is not good, but I want to tell you I care about you. May I can't express my feeling sometimes, but I'll tell you with my smile. Hope you enjoy yourself in Beijing."

Later, we were lying in bed, face to face, when Sen asked if I'd ever consider moving to Beijing to be with him. I didn't know what to do. Part of me had fantasized about a future together with Sen. I could see us together in Beijing, doing the things couples do together—shopping at the local markets, eating at Sen's favorite restaurants, going out for drinks with his friends. But there was another part of me that wondered if I'd miss out on something if I stopped wandering. *How would I know when it was time to be still?*

How would I know?

I smiled at Sen, then leaned in and kissed him. Then, I pulled back and saw him smiling back at me. I don't quite remember what I said after that, but I remember thinking about this invitation to move to Beijing every day during my ten-day trip around Yunnan Province. I remember Sen's words looping around in my head, his smile, this kiss, the hotel room around us. I remember my mind zooming out on this memory of us lying together, face to face, smiling like a couple of fools. I also remember being afraid that if I stopped wandering and started something new with Sen, I'd never again have the opportunity to follow the rambling wanderlust out into the unknown. That wanderlust had propelled me to venture beyond my comfort zone and had taught me to appreciate the beauty of the world around me. I still felt that I had more to learn. More to experience. More to see and do.

~

I can picture the room described in Baldwin's book. I can see the two windows covered in cleaning polish, the curls of torn-off wallpaper littering the floor, the violin resting on the table. I can see the morning sun filtering in the windows and the shadows of people passing through the courtyard outside the room. I can also feel this sense of being watched described by David in the book, this idea that the two windows were eyes looking in on him and Giovanni and what they were doing in that room. I felt the same way when I first came out, as if the whole world were watching me.

But I also feel something else when picturing Giovanni's room. I feel love, safety, joy. If all the newspapers and bottles and other clutter were stripped away, the room feels intimate and comfortable to me. Instead of a room where the sunlight and windows and everything else pose a threat, the room becomes a sanctuary. A place to escape the rest of the world.

I have a similar relationship with the rooms I've loved and been loved in. I remember everything on the walls of the dorm room where I had my first kiss. I remember the specific way the moonlight filtered into the bedroom of my first apartment while I lay in my twin-size bed with my first boyfriend. I can tell you so much about the coffee shop where I first met my husband. I can describe these rooms better than I can describe some of the people I've met over the years. Part of this has to do with my training first as a soldier who must scan his surroundings for threats and second as a journalist who must document what he sees around him. But I also have fond memories of these rooms because they were the only places I felt safe enough to truly be myself. These neat little boxes with doors and walls to close out the chaotic world. I came to associate so many of these rooms with security and my own acceptance of my sexuality. When I started wandering the world like a sailor, the temporary apartments where I lived while teaching and the hotel and hostel rooms where I laid my head while traveling took on an even greater meaning. I came to see these rooms as the only places someone could see the real me and not some anonymous wandering guy trying to please everyone in order to figure out where he belonged. This was especially true in China, where I often felt I had to project a more confident, independent man when I was in public, even though I often worried I didn't have the skills necessary to live the kind of life I wanted to live.

~

Kunming was crowded. I found a bed at a hostel called Hump. (I didn't entertain the action suggested by the name, nor did I pay attention to whether or not the travelers staying there were all having sex around me. I just liked the name.) I mostly kept to myself and spent a couple days pushing my way through throngs of strangers packing the streets around the city. I deployed a technique called darting, where I would zip effortlessly through a crowd, zigging left and zagging right, until I had found my way past all the people with ease. It was a maneuver I could do only when I was alone since I didn't have to worry about letting anyone or anything slow me down. *Get in, get out, move on.*

Dali, my second stop, was quieter, sleepy even, so I didn't have to deploy much darting. Instead, I drifted aimlessly down the streets. I found a hostel with cartoon bluebirds painted onto the shutters near the old city center. Since the universities in the area hadn't finished yet, the hostel was empty, and I had a room that normally slept five people to myself for the entire three days I was there. On my third day in Dali, I rented a bike and pedaled out to the ear-shaped lake near the town. I had heard that the lake used to be a sanctuary for wayward foreigners who would gather around it, smoke weed, and laze about all day with little on their minds. I'd also heard that the government had gotten tired of all these wayward foreigners and had cleaned up the area a few years before my arrival.

I had a hard time finding the path suggested in my guidebook because my normally functioning sense of direction seemed to be off. So, by the time I got to the lake, I was too tired and frustrated to hop on a ferry and check out the ruins and old temples surrounding the lake. Instead, I sat in a shady spot and thought about Sen. I wondered what he was doing back in Beijing. I wondered what he'd be doing if I were there. I wondered what life would even look like if I just stopped moving, if I stayed still and settled into one place. My trip had been all about myself, a solo adventure I had told myself I needed to go on in order to understand something about the person I'd become in China, but every day I thought about Sen. I thought about him while walking the old streets, while watching the paper lanterns swaying in the wind, even while taking sips from a lukewarm beer in the courtyards outside my hostels. Each time he popped into my mind I paused and wondered whether it was time to stop living so much for myself.

This feeling dissipated a bit when I got to Lijiang, an old city of cobbled streets and gushing canals north of Dali. The shuttle van from Dali dropped me off near Old Market Square in the old part of Lijiang, and I walked through the rain to a popular guesthouse that my guidebook recommended. I had chosen the guesthouse because it hosted communal, family-style dinners in the evenings, and after getting bombarded by thoughts of Sen while biking outside Dali, I wanted to surround myself with other travelers who could distract me from thinking about him.

It rained for the two days I was in Lijiang, so I stuck to wandering the cobbled streets of the old city and spent my afternoons around the fireplace at the hostel. At the communal dinners, I met other travelers and gathered information about the trails through Tiger Leaping Gorge. One guy had just returned from hiking the Gorge trail, and when I asked him about it, he said, "It was muddy." He then asked if I had hiking boots, and when I shook my head, he got up from the table, went to his bunk in the back of the hostel, and returned a moment later with a pair.

"You'll need these," he said, handing me the boots.

After hearing from other travelers about their hike through the Gorge, my heart was set on hiking it. I decided to follow a group of students from Minnesota to Shangri-la to spend a day waiting out the rain there and then loop back to hike Tiger Leaping Gorge for three days before catching a bus back to Kunming for my flight.

In Shangri-la, I met Paulina, a Polish woman traveling alone, and that evening—over yak hotpot—she proposed a plan to visit Baishuitai, a plateau of limestone deposits featuring glittering pools of water. "Supposed to be beautiful," she said. "Want to check it out with me?" My guidebook said it is possible to go from Baishuitai to the trail up to Tiger Leaping Gorge, going the opposite way most travelers do. My instinct was to stick to my original plan of hiking the Gorge the next day, but something about Pauline's eyes gave me pause. I could sense her loneliness. She needed a travel companion. But there was something else in those eyes as well. Baishuitai wasn't a well-visited place, so I sensed that Paulina needed someone else to accompany her so she could feel safe venturing off the well-beaten path. I didn't mind taking on this role, especially considering that I'd been looking for a travel companion as well.

The plan was for us to take a four-hour bus through the mountains to reach Baishuitai and then hike part of the trail before sundown. Then, we would hike the rest of the trail the following day, which would give me time to get back to Kunming to catch my flight. When we got off the bus in Baishuitai, we went to an information booth along the side of the road to ask about directions to the Tiger Leaping Gorge trail. Inside the booth a teenager was reading a magazine. Paulina's Mandarin was decent—much better than mine—so she asked the teen about the pass.

"He says the pass is closed," Paulina said back to me after talking to the teen. "We'll have to stay here tonight, and in the morning, we can catch a bus back to Shangri-la."

Bullshit, I thought, looking out over the mountain valley in front of us. That was the kind of thing that happened all the time in China—locals gave incorrect information in order to con gullible foreigners into spending money. After learning from past experiences—such as when I got conned into an expensive tuk-tuk ride in Beijing during the Harvest Festival—I knew to trust my own instincts and the information from the guidebook and to ignore anything I thought sounded fishy.

I was upset, not at Paulina for suggesting we come to Baishuitai but at myself for not trusting my own instincts and letting my own loneliness dictate my actions. I felt as if I'd betrayed the very self I'd been working on all these years, this independent man unburdened by others, this drifting expatriate pretending he knew what he was doing. Only later—years after leaving China and returning to the U.S.—did I recognize this act of accompanying Paulina to Baishuitai as one of my first steps in giving up my wandering-sailor life.

I never made it to Tiger Leaping Gorge. We took a bus back to Shangri-la, and then I took another bus to Kunming to catch my flight. But that evening, after spending less than an hour admiring the limestone terraces and the white-water pools, we wandered around the village and then rented a room in a hostel across the street from the terraces, the only travelers at the hostel. There weren't any restaurants in the village, but the owner of the hostel had chickens, so we bought one from her and asked her to prepare a few dishes for us. We ate our dinner on a picnic table outside the hostel and then watched the sun set behind the mountains before heading up to our room. Just before climbing into our creaky beds, we realized that the door didn't have a lock, so we pushed one of the empty beds up against it in case anyone tried to get in during the night. Paulina fell asleep right away, but I lay awake tossing and turning, thinking about how unsafe I felt in that room. I tried to close my eyes and picture a different room—the bedroom I shared with my brother in the farmhouse I grew up in or the hotel room in Winnipeg where I said *I love you* to a boyfriend for the first time—but lying there on that thin mattress in that hostel room without a lock on the door, all I could think about was how someone could easily break into our room and harm us. Every time the hostel owner's dog barked, my eyes shot open and my body stiffened. I lay there wide awake, my ears perked up, waiting to hear the crunch of gravel underfoot, the thump of boots climbing the steps to our room, the sharp crack of the door being kicked in.

～

On our second day in the hotel room in Beijing, I asked Sen to teach me how to write his name. I handed him the pocket notebook I always kept with me while traveling, and he swiftly drew two beautiful characters—these wispy butterflies ready to float off the page.

"Forest," he said, pointing at the second character.

I looked where he was pointing and saw three smaller characters that looked like trees—two on the bottom and one stacked on top. His given name meant "forest" in English.

"Watch," he said, and I watched as he wrote his name again, this time slowly drawing each stroke and looking over at me to see whether I was paying attention.

When he handed the notebook and pen to me, I clumsily scratched out a few lines that looked nothing like Sen's characters. I wasn't great at writing Chinese characters, but I'd taken a Chinese calligraphy class in college and knew the importance of each stroke and why doing them in a certain order mattered. Still, my fingers couldn't make the characters look like the beautiful butterflies Sen created. My characters looked like these thick-limbed monsters someone hastily stitched together. When I looked up at Sen for his approval, he just smiled and ran his hand along my cheek.

With Sen, all I have are these rooms—the room in the club where we meet, the second-floor lounge where I leaned in to kiss him, the online "room" I pretended we were in when we chatted on QQ, the hotel room where we spent the better part of three days. Each one sealed off and placed together into this memory palace I've created in my mind. Every now and then, I like to toss open the door and walk through those rooms, touching the tapestries and knocking on the faux-wooden furniture, remembering the time Sen and I spent together and how much he helped me reckon with the wandering lifestyle I'd been living.

～

I am writing this during a two-week cold snap that has left the panes of the storm windows in my office frosted over. The office is on the second floor of this old four-square house I bought with my husband. One of the windows overlooks the backyard where, in the summer, we grow tomatoes and wildflowers and try to keep pests from eating the fruit on our lone apple tree. Shivering in my cold office, I try to look through the frost, to remind myself of those summer days, but the feathered layers of ice crystals swirled onto most of the pane obstruct my view.

For the last year of lockdown due to a global pandemic, I have been teaching from my home office while an old pug snores at my feet and an old cat dawdles back and forth in front of my computer screen. My husband works in the next room. When he leads a meeting, I close the door to my office to shut out his voice. With the door closed, I feel a little claustrophobic; the walls seem a little bit closer each day. Some days the walls give off a heat that I find comforting. Other days I feel scorched by these flames. I want to run across the barren fields near the farm where I grew up, wild and unencumbered, just to get away from these rooms I've been trapped in for the past year. But I can't. It is too cold for such foolishness and too dangerous for reckless wandering. Instead, I take brief walks around my neighborhood with the pug and make weekly runs to the store for groceries. For the most part, I sit in this room speaking to a screen of black boxes and thinking about this wandering young man who used to drift from place to place with little regard for what or who he left behind.

I open my email and type Sen's name into my inbox's search field. Up pop seventeen emails. Shortly after my trip through Yunnan Province, I took a job at a tribal college ninety miles north of my hometown in North Dakota. I lived fourteen miles from the Canadian border, in an apartment across from a Walmart at the edge of town. Sen and I emailed periodically. He updated me on his life in Beijing, and I told him about my new job and my family nearby. He sent me emails on Thanksgiving and New Year's and on Chinese Valentine's Day. In one email, he remarked that he sometimes thought about the three days we spent together in Beijing. *It's warmth*, he concluded. In another, he asked for my address in the U.S., and when I responded he sent back an aerial screenshot of my apartment building in North Dakota. The screenshot was a little blurry, but I could make out the brick building where I lived at the time. I'm not sure what Sen did with this screenshot, but for a while I imagined him looking at that screenshot and wondering what I was doing inside my apartment, what I was thinking, how I was feeling, whether I ever thought about him and the life we could have had in Beijing.

I did, occasionally.

I click the button to start a new email to Sen, knowing that my email will probably come back undelivered. The last email from him was dated eight years earlier and his email address was probably deactivated long ago. Still, I want to ask him about his life and tell him that even though meeting him helped me recognize how aimless I felt wandering from place to place, I still let wanderlust guide me for a few years after leaving China. I wandered through other places and, for a time, speculated if I'd always be this wandering sailor. *Maybe I wasn't meant to be still*, I thought at the time. *Maybe my path in life is to always be wandering, this modern-day disciple always looking for something better and more exciting.*

I type a bit of that into the message field and then sit back and stare at what I've written. Around me, I can feel the heat of my office walls pushing against me, the frost of the windows keeping me from looking out. I want to latch onto this message I'm sending out into the ether, to grab hold of it and let myself be flung, adrift in the wild again.

I reach out and wait for the message to carry me away.

Finish Line

I've never been very good at finishing things, so let me just say up front how this ends: A week after watching a pair of "goat farmers"-slash-boyfriends win the twenty-first season of *The Amazing Race* and feeling a renewed sense of hope about my relationship, my boyfriend of fifteen months and I broke up when I told him I didn't love him anymore.

After I said it, I watched the tears pool in the corners of his eyes. He turned to gather the overnight bag he always used when he visited me for the weekend. On his way out, he slammed my apartment door and then ran down the wooden back stairs. I should have just let him go, but something inside me told me to try to explain myself. I followed him down the stairs and out to the street, trying to get him to talk. He wanted nothing to do with me. He climbed into his car and sped away.

Earlier that fall, I had convinced my boyfriend, John, to watch *The Amazing Race* with me. The basic premise of the show is that pairs race around the world (usually to eight to ten countries on four or more continents) navigating new locations, finding clues, and avoiding elimination. On each leg of the race, teams must complete challenges (such as searching among four hundred sandcastles on a beach in Indonesia or launching watermelons at a suit of armor in England) to get clues to another location and eventually to the pit stop at the end of the leg. The last team to check in at the pit stop is (usually) eliminated. On the final leg, the first team to jump onto the finish mat wins a million dollars.

The only openly queer team on season 21 was a couple named Josh and Brent (aka the Beekman Boys). They owned a goat farm in upstate New York. Josh was also a writer whose memoir about being a drag queen in New York I admired. When I heard that he was going to be competing in the race with his boyfriend, they instantly became my favorite team. They were smart and well-adjusted and seemed to enjoy each other's company. But they were also flawed. They struggled with some of the physical challenges. Many of the other teams wrote them off as real contenders after they finished last in the fifth leg of the race, a non-elimination leg. After that, they continued to struggle, coming in second-to-last in legs six through eleven. Still, I admired their perseverance, their determination, how they didn't let the pressures of the race influence their relationship. Even after finishing second-to-last, they kept trying, picking themselves up leg after leg and soldiering on. I came to see Josh and Brent as hapless underdogs worth cheering on but also as a model for my relationship with John. They were a real, queer couple—something I didn't have many examples of at the time, in real life or in popular culture, but needed to see to help me visualize what my relationship with John could be.

Before watching season 21, I had convinced myself that John and I weren't compatible. We got along fine, but I wasn't ready to commit myself to building a future with him. I wanted to date other people. I just couldn't figure out the right way to break up with him. I felt as if I were in this strange limbo, hanging onto a relationship I knew wasn't going to work, not knowing how to get out of it. I realize now how unfair this was to him, but at the time I was too emotionally immature to know how to end a relationship. Instead of being honest about how I felt, I continued to hang on while we watched *The Amazing Race* that fall, week after week, hoping *something* would happen to change how I felt.

In the final leg of season 21, the race came down to Josh and Brent and a pair of Chippendales dancers named Jaymes and James (And yes, their team photo pictured them shirtless with backpacks and the requisite bow tie and shirt-cuffs). The boyfriends finished the final challenge first, just ahead of the dancers. They caught a taxi to Gotham Hall, where they ran past the eight eliminated teams and stepped onto a big red mat placed at the finish line. Josh fell to his knees, then rose, grasped Brent's head with both hands, and kissed him passionately—the first kiss between two men I could remember seeing on the show. Then, the show's host stepped forward and declared them the winners.

When Josh and Brent burst through the doors of Gotham Hall, John and I jumped up off the couch in disbelief. *They actually pulled it off*, I half-yelled. I hugged John, and we held each other for a moment, lost in the joy of seeing our favorite team succeed. I gave John a quick peck on the lips and then leaped around my living room like some crazy fool. Once the initial shock wore off and we sat back down, I looked over at John and felt a surge of hope and possibility. If Josh and Brent could pull off such a spectacular upset, maybe we could make our battered relationship work. We just needed to keep going, keep trying, keep believing in ourselves and what we'd built together.

A week later, that feeling faded. John asked whether I still loved him and, instead of lying and saying that I did, I surprised myself by actually admitting what I'd been avoiding saying for so long—that I just didn't love him anymore. Once the words came out, I couldn't take them back, so I let them float in front of me, like a fine mist, as John grabbed his bag and stormed out my apartment door. There was no happy ending where I caught up with John, explained myself, and then kissed him as Josh had kissed Brent at the end of season 21—deeply, passionately, with both hands. Instead, there was just me stumbling down the stairs, calling for John to stop, to wait, to let me explain myself, before making it to the street and watching John's car turn the corner and drive away.

A One-Time Thing

It should have been a one-time thing. We'd hooked up one night in December, shortly after I broke up with my boyfriend, and something about the whole encounter left me feeling ravenous and greedy like a starved bear. It started when we were making out on my bed. A few minutes in, this guy (I'll call him Alex) pulled away from me and said, "I feel like I'm being devoured," and I smiled, apologized, and told him that I could be a little aggressive sometimes. I didn't say anything about this hunger that had been building inside me or how, since my boyfriend, I'd been noticing that hunger more and more. I just tried to hold a little bit back while I continued kissing him.

After, we talked about our master's degree programs while we got dressed, and I thought about the details of his life he was doling out, how willing he was to share so much with me. I couldn't help but admire how open and unafraid Alex was. I was used to keeping everything in, hiding the details of my life so they couldn't be used against me.

That should have been the last I heard from him, but a few nights later I got a message inviting me to a local bar for a drink. I didn't even hesitate before saying yes. As I walked to the bar, I thought of his invitation as a sign that he wanted more than just a one-time thing. *What if he was actually smart and charming and easy to talk to outside my bedroom? What if this turned into something more?* I was like that when I first started using the hookup apps. Sex was never just about physical desire. I thought every message, every flirty quip, every hookup held the possibility of a whole new world opening to me. And who was I to turn my back on all that possibility?

At the bar, I looked around and quickly spotted Alex at a high-top across the room. He wore skinny jeans, which I found gross on most people but on him seemed just right, and a collared shirt that fit snugly around his biceps. It was one of those shirts where it was difficult to tell what color it was because the fabric seemed to shimmer and shift in the light. One moment it was teal, then he shifted, and it turned a purply blue. I smiled walking across the bar, happy that my memory of him from a few nights earlier was correct, that I hadn't imagined how attractive he was.

When I got to his table, Alex introduced me to his friends sitting across from him—a young woman with blonde highlights, who I'll call Amy, and a young guy with dark hair and this goofy, far-off look in his eyes. I shook their hands and sat down next to Alex.

For a while, I listened to Alex chat with his friends, thinking that maybe this had been a mistake. I wasn't expecting his friends to be there. I'd thought I would have him all to myself, that I'd be able to get more details about who he was over a beer or two. I had been hoping for something a little more intimate. Instead, I ordered a beer and sat back and listened to them talk, feeling a little bit like a third wheel.

When his friends snuck out for a smoke, I took the opportunity to come clean.

"My name isn't really John," I said, looking away from Alex quickly.

When we first met on the hookup app, I had introduced myself as "John" because I was still resistant to giving away too much online. I was new to the hookup apps, and I didn't know what to expect, so I kept as much as I could close to the chest. But, seeing Alex in the bar and hearing him talk with his friends, I felt that I needed to be more open and honest about myself. He was giving so much to me, and I was still holding back.

"That's OK," Alex responded to my confession, as if it was no big deal.

I wasn't sure what to make of this nonchalant attitude. Alex was clearly much more comfortable with himself than I was. I admired his confidence, this ability to just lay himself bare so easily. It made it easy to like him. I, on the other hand, felt reluctant to reveal too much, to let others into my life. It was a product of the wandering-sailor life I lived for so long, where I didn't want to give too much away because I wasn't sure how long I'd stay in one place.

Years earlier, when I was thinking about whether to stay in China and start a relationship with a man there, I had learned that I needed to start sharing more of myself with others and stop holding so much about myself in. I had been working on being more open with others, trusting that what I shared with them would help me build more intimate, lasting relationships. It was a process I was still working on.

I looked at Alex and smiled, glad that my little lie wasn't a deal-breaker for him. He smiled back and rubbed my forearm gently.

"I'm glad you came," he said.

"Me too," I replied, looking away quickly because I didn't want him to see too much of this goofball smile I had plastered to my face after realizing that he was just as charming as I had feared.

We talked about his friends, his high school years. I opened up and told Alex about my job and how I'd spent a few years traveling, trying to figure out who I was. He nodded and took a swig from his beer. He mentioned how awkward he felt staying with his parents and how much he hated staying in his old bedroom. *So much has changed*, he said, and I nodded because I understood. I felt the same way when I went home.

"Maybe I could stay with you tonight?" Alex said, smiling.

I was too charmed to realize how up-front Alex's request was, how bold it seemed for him to just ask for what he wanted. I should have been a little bit coyer with my response, but I was trying to put myself out there more and not turn away from something that could become meaningful. So, I nodded and said, "I'd like that," and gently placed my hand on Alex's thigh.

Eventually, Alex's friends came back, and they continued catching up. I listened to them, chiming in every now and then, my hand resting on Alex's thigh the entire time. After a while, we decided to move to the outdoor patio. I was already a few beers in, so the whole world around me felt warm and fuzzy. I ordered another beer and settled into a patio chair next to Alex. In my past relationships, it had taken a while to really get a feeling for whether or not a relationship had legs. This felt different. It felt much more organic. I was clearly getting attached to Alex, but I told myself that that was all right. Maybe that was just how relationships worked in the era of hookup apps.

We were on the patio for an hour when a truck pulled up right next to us. Alex looked over at the truck, then got up and approached the driver's side, where the guy behind the wheel had rolled down the window. At first, I thought it was just another one of Alex's friends, but the more I watched, the more I realized that this man was something else. Alex stood next to the truck laughing and smiling at the man. He was clearly flirting. Something was going on between them, but I couldn't quite figure it out. I sat back in my chair, watching them, and tried not to look hurt. Alex and I weren't boyfriends. We weren't dating. We were nothing more than two guys who had hooked up. Why then did it hurt to see him standing there flirting with this other man? Why did I feel that pain deep down in my stomach where I often pushed my feelings because I'd learned that it wasn't right for queer men to be so open about what they desired? What was I feeling?

I got up and went to the restroom, where I stood before the mirror and tried to figure out what was happening, why I felt so torn and twisted inside, why it hurt so much. When I got back to the patio, Alex was gone and so was the truck. I looked around to see if he was somewhere else on the patio or at the bar, but I didn't see him. I took out my phone, opened the app, and sent him a message.

Where'd you go? I wrote and then just stared at those three words for a few minutes, waiting for him to reply. *Was this just what he did, hopped between men so nonchalantly with little regard for how it made them feel?* In my head, I imagined that this guy with the truck was just one of many guys Alex hooked up while he was home. I wanted to be OK with this sex-positive version of Alex I'd created in my head, but I was too hurt to feel anything but anger and shame from leaving myself exposed. I'd felt the brush-off from men before, but something about this time stung more deeply. It could have been that I'd finally opened myself up to someone and let myself believe that what I had with Alex could be more than just sex. I also felt this sense of shame at letting myself fall for him in front of his friends. They probably thought I was a fool.

I could feel Amy watching me. She must have known what was going on. She had probably seen Alex bring hookups to the bar before, only to run off with someone else. She reached over, touched my forearm, and smiled, and I knew I was correct in assuming that Alex was hooking up with someone else. She opened her mouth slightly, but nothing came out.

After a few minutes and no response from Alex, I tucked the phone back into my pocket and sat stewing in my own self-loathing. I should have left then, slipped away to feel bad for myself alone. But I couldn't. Amy clearly felt sorry for me and felt that she needed to make right what Alex had done.

"Come on," Amy said to me. "We're switching bars."

I took her hand, and she led me across the street and down an alley to another bar. I was a little drunk at this point and feeling pretty sorry for myself, so I let myself be pulled along. At the new bar, Amy sat me down in a booth, and a moment later a glass of beer appeared before me. I sat in that booth with these people I didn't really know, nursing a beer I didn't really want, trying to ignore the hurt I didn't know how to soothe. At some point, Alex just appeared across the table from me, unchanged, beer in hand, still handsome and charming as all hell. I looked at him and felt this hot anger burning behind my eyes. I may have asked where he'd been. I may have said something about spending the night. I may have said nothing at all and just stared at him. After a little while, probably noticing how much of a nuisance I'd become and figuring it was best to just be honest with me, Alex leaned across the table and said, "I think you should leave."

I did. I got up from the booth and stumbled out of the bar. I was ashamed of how I'd acted, how I'd turned into this animal just pawing at what he wanted. *Who* was *that?* I asked myself later, alone in my apartment, licking my wounds. *Where did that guy come from?* A few days after Alex asked me to leave the bar, I sent him a message apologizing for my behavior. He, of course, accepted my apology as if it was no big deal, like he'd seen it all before.

I saw Alex a few years later, while we were both crammed shoulder to shoulder at an outdoor concert. We locked eyes, and, for a moment, this image of us fucking in my tent back at the campground flashed into my head. But then I quickly looked away—still embarrassed by my drunken behavior that night, still wounded by his nonchalance and charm—and I shook away that image of us hooking up again. I reminded myself that it was always meant to be a one-time thing.

When I got to my apartment after leaving Alex at the bar, I reached into my back pocket and realized my wallet was missing. It must have fallen out on the walk home. I turned around and left the apartment, still a little wobbly from the beer, and lunged down the street toward the bar, retracing my steps. I probably looked a little insane ambling along, looking at my feet, still a little numb from everything that had happened that evening. I wish I could say that I didn't recognize this man drifting along, misty-eyed and ambivalent about so much of the world around him. But I can't. I knew this wandering fool, this heartbroken boy, this stumbling bear, this man looking for what he'd lost. I knew him all too well.

Thirst & Trap

I was in bed, an old pug snoring next to me, two cats curled at the foot of the bed, my husband at my side checking his fantasy baseball league on his iPad, when the obituary for my first thirst-trap crush came sliding up my Facebook feed. I froze and stared at the attached photo. He looked the same, maybe a little wider in the face, a little thicker neck. I clicked on the link and scrolled through the details. He was an only child, which I knew. He was only thirty-nine, a year older than me, which I didn't know. We'd never talked about our ages.

The obituary didn't say anything about a husband or partner.

Below the link a shared friend had posted a comment saying that he'd talked to the family. My crush's parents were devastated. They had Christmas presents wrapped and waiting under the tree. The friend assured everyone that it wasn't suicide. He had fallen and hit his head and was dead for several days before anyone found him.

Seeing the obituary reminded me of how fascinated I was with thirst traps when I first started online dating in 2011. A thirst trap was a provocative photo someone posted online to attract attention. Shirtless men holding food or cute animals, grinning widely for the camera. Guys in their underwear looking pensively off-camera, as if lost in thought. Men lying in bed with perfectly coifed hair, the photo cut off in just the right place to leave enough to the imagination. They were everywhere, begging me to stop and look and linger.

At first, these thirst traps seemed fake, needy, manipulative even. They were meant to lure us away from our lives, to prey on our never-ending quest for the desirable, to make us believe that everything in life can be immaculately staged and perfectly posed. I had just spent two years in China, a country obsessed with image and appearances, and the showiness of thirst traps gave me the same hollow feeling I'd get while staring at something I knew wasn't as good as it looked.

Thirst traps made me feel sort of empty inside.

But there was also something captivating about how the thirst traps presented their subjects, how the good ones seemed to offer a snapshot of perfection in the minute it took to take them. I approached looking at thirst traps the same way I did those Magic Eye 3D posters I'd stared at as a kid. If I stared long enough, I believed, I could see something real in those thirst traps. One day it would just appear like the sharks and butterflies and other hidden images did. I just needed to look at them long enough.

I was especially curious about the thirst traps local men posted on their dating profiles. The man from the obituary was one of the first I remember stopping and lingering over. In the man's photo, he stood in front of a shower curtain, his bare shoulders and chest just visible, his wet hair swept back from his face, the corner of his mouth raised in a smirk. He was handsome, in a boy-next-door kind of way. I stared at the trap for a while and then clicked into his profile and sent him a message. I normally wasn't so bold, but something about the trap's allure gave me courage. To my surprise, the man responded, and after a few flirty quips back and forth, he introduced himself as Michael.

For a week, Michael and I volleyed messages back and forth. We chatted about dating in a small city and our favorite novels and what we liked and disliked about *The Walking Dead*. He told me about being an only child, and I told him what it was like being the oldest of six. We shared our stories of growing up and coming out. He had a Yorkshire terrier named Winston and I had just rescued a pug named Amos, so we sent each other dozens of photos of our pets in various situations. Chatting with him felt comfortable, safe. At times it even felt real, like we were in the same room.

Eventually, I felt comfortable enough to send my own version of a thirst trap, one of me lying on my couch with my arm over my head and Amos snuggled at my side. From there we moved to talking on the phone. The first time we talked, I nervously paced my living room trying to think of what I could say to make myself sound authentic and worth meeting in person. I wanted to convince him that I was more than just what he saw in that thirst trap. At the same time, I was accumulating enough evidence to convince myself that what I saw in his thirst trap was real. I wanted to believe Michael, but I also felt it was difficult to portray yourself authentically online, and I was suspicious of anything that seemed overly manufactured and posed. I had heard about catfishing, where someone pretends to be someone else online, so I was protecting myself in case Michael's thirst trap was all just a façade.

One night, a couple weeks after we'd started chatting, I was out walking Amos, and I stopped in front of a house to watch a woman hang shelves in her living room. From all the unpacked boxes I could see through the window, it seemed like the woman had just moved in, and seeing her putting up shelves and settle into her house, I found myself thinking about all the scenes of domestic life I'd seen on television and in movies. I thought about buying a house with someone, about walking our dogs together around our new neighborhood, about hanging shelves and making dinner and curling up in each other's arms in front of the television. I wanted all of that, and even though we'd been chatting for only a few weeks, I felt that Michael wanted that as well. Our weeks of chatting and texting had started to slowly fill in the space around that thirst trap, and seeing this woman settle into her new home made me long for a life together with someone. All I needed to do was convince Michael to meet me in person.

When I got back to my apartment, I sent Michael a message asking whether he wanted to get coffee. He agreed, and we made arrangements for our first date. We would meet on a Sunday afternoon at a coffee shop in a strip mall on the north side of town.

On the day of our scheduled date, I ended up getting delayed coming back to town and had to cancel at the last minute. Michael didn't seem to mind when I called to reschedule.

"It's OK," he replied when I canceled. "I like to take things slow."

When I tried to set up a new date, he was noncommittal, mentioning work or other obligations, and I thought that I'd missed my chance.

Still, I kept trying. I suggested crowded bars and quiet coffee shops, weeknights, afternoons, morning coffee. Nothing stuck, and after a few failed attempts, I started to believe that he'd lost interest. For a week, I teetered between believing I could make that imagined future of buying a house and walking our dogs together a reality and believing that nothing of what I'd learned about Michael was real. He wasn't this cute, boy-next-door type. He didn't watch *The Walking Dead*. There probably wasn't even a dog named Winston. It was all fake, as I'd initially imaged thirst traps to be.

Just when I was about to give up, Michael texted with a new piece of bait. Our state was about to vote on a constitutional amendment defining marriage as only between one man and one woman, ensuring that same-sex marriage would become illegal.

"If the amendment fails," Michael wrote, "I will give you a kiss."

I was stuck inside his trap, and, instead of admitting to myself that he was just stringing me along, I once again took his bait. When the amendment failed, I casually brought up the kiss in a text message, hoping this would finally lead to us meeting. But Michael just brushed it off. The skeptical part of me was saying *give up, move on*, but the hopeful part still believed that there was something real between us. I just needed to wait a little longer, to keep looking for the hidden butterflies that were bound to appear.

I didn't hear from Michael for a week, and then, out of nowhere, I saw a post on his Facebook page saying that he'd met the man of his dreams and that they were engaged to be married. I was blindsided. All this time he'd had someone else. He was just casting his line out, seeing if anything new caught his eye.

I stared at Michael's post and tried to figure out what had happened, where this other guy had come from. I was right there, right in front of him (figuratively—after a month and a half of chatting back and forth, we had still never met in person), yet I wasn't able to make him see me. I'd spent all this time looking for something real in Michael, but I'd failed to think about how I could make myself more visible, more desirable, more worthy of meeting in person. I'd failed to consider how weak my own thirst trap was.

I should have ended it there and tried to forget about Michael, but instead, I sent him one last message explaining how hurt I was hearing about this other guy. In my head, I composed a message that was filled with fury and frustration. I wanted to say something about hope and manipulation and how deceptive it was making people believe in a facade. Mostly, I wanted him to feel bad about leading me on. But when I actually wrote the message, none of that anger came out. Instead, I wrote, *I hope you find what you are looking for*, even though I wasn't entirely sure I believed that.

Looking back on that time now, I am embarrassed by how intense this desire to see something real in Michael had been and how feverishly I had wanted him to see me. All those thirst traps had made me believe that I could be seen online the way I wanted to be seen if I posed the right way and said the right things and made people stop and linger over my image.

Seeing Michael's obituary reminded me of the only time I'd ever seen him in person. It was years after we'd first chatted online. We hadn't kept in touch, but when I saw him, I recognized him immediately. And I think he recognized me, too. We caught each other's eye in passing, and for a moment I wondered whether he'd stop and smile and ask about Amos or whether I was still watching *The Walking Dead*, and we'd start over what we'd begun so many years before.

I heard from Michael once more after that. A few years after we first chatted online, I received a text from him asking to borrow money. It was an odd thing to text someone you'd never actually met in person. But, after reading it, I wondered whether Michael *had* felt a real connection with me, one he felt was strong enough for him to consider reaching out and asking for money. *Could that have been possible?* I thought. *Or was I just falling for another one of his traps?*

I never responded to the text.

"What's wrong?" my husband asked when he noticed me staring at the wall, lost in thought after reading Michael's obituary.

I looked over at him and tried to smile. I couldn't help but feel sad about Michael. I wanted to know whether he'd lived a happy life, whether he'd actually found what he was looking for. Days later, I went back to the obituary and scanned it for clues. He was survived by Winston, the obituary said, as well as many aunts and uncles and cousins and friends. The comments under the obituary were filled with descriptions of Michael as a kind, lovable guy. A neighbor commented about Michael always holding the door open for her. Someone wrote about always chatting with Michael in the break room at their work, even though he didn't know Michael's name. One comment in particular caught my eye because it seemed to express my own experience interacting with Michael online. "I had not known Michael long but [as] soon as we met we were friends," the comment read. "We seemed to be able to talk to each other about anything."

The obituary didn't say anything about a husband or partner.

False Start

It was dusk the first time I viewed my first house, so there was a lot I didn't notice. I didn't notice the dent in the back wall of the garage where the neighbor had backed his car into it and rippled the siding. I didn't notice the missing heating grate in the living room or the unfinished electric socket behind the kitchen hutch or the long-gone storm window in the dining room. I didn't notice the piece of drywall missing at the back of the bedroom closet, leaving an opening I imagined bats flying through. When I looked at the house number, I didn't notice that flipping the two nines would have revealed the symbol of the devil. (I still have dreams of those nines swiveling around slowly—like they do in scary movies—and bursting into 666-shaped flames.) Most important, I didn't notice the way my boyfriend John looked at me when I talked about the house and how he imagined a future of us living together there.

In my head, I had this superficial image of home buying, where I'd meet a guy at a coffee shop or a poetry reading, fall in love, and then start looking for the perfect house together, something with big windows and hardwood floors and a spacious yard for a dog and a vegetable garden. We'd browse listings, attend open houses, follow our realtor through doorways and stand before rooms, holding hands and imagining our future together.

In reality, I had convinced myself that John and I weren't meant to be together, but I still wanted to move on to the next stage of my life, so one day I emailed a realtor and asked her to show me a few places.

Shortly after putting in an offer on that first house, John brought up the possibility of us moving in together. I didn't respond right away. John was kind and gentle and ready to settle down, but I had long since convinced myself that we were different people looking for different things. When he brought up moving in together a second time, I shrugged it off and changed the subject. I realized then that I was more committed to buying a house than I was to my boyfriend, so, three weeks before I closed on my house, we broke up.

~

The G.I. Bill was originally called the Servicemen's Readjustment Act of 1944. It was created to help World War II veterans buy homes and reintegrate after the war. When I first read this while combing through information about VA home loans, I paused after the word *readjustment*. To *readjust* was to adapt or change (once again) because of a new environment. *Readjustment*, therefore, was the process of making that change.

I had long since readjusted from the year I spent in Iraq with the Army in 2003 and 2004, but ten years after returning from that war, I had recognized that my life needed readjusting once again. I had a comfortable job and friends who still made me happy, but my life still felt empty. I felt too much like the wayward sailor I had pretended to be during my twenties. I was looking for something to move me beyond this stage of my life, and I knew owning a house meant something. It came with a certain power, and because of the G.I. Bill and the VA home loan program, I felt that power was within reach.

But I had never thought of buying a house as an adjustment. I just thought it was a natural part of being an adult in America, something one could transition to with ease. No need to change anything about who I was or how I was living. I could slide right into this new life, no adjustment necessary.

~

I moved into my house a few days after Christmas, on a sunny winter day. After arranging my tiny smattering of furniture, I walked through my house and did a quick inventory of everything the previous owner had left behind. I felt like I'd been dropped into this life-in-progress, as if I were in some video game with the homeowner starting pack already installed and all I really needed to do was continue what the previous owner had already begun.

A month before closing, the previous owner had sent my realtor a list of items he was willing to include in the sale of the house—a military-style tanker desk, a leather couch, something he called a "permanent" Christmas tree (meaning a fake tree in a box)—and a second list with expensive items he wanted to sell—a two-hundred-dollar lawn mower, a one-year-old leaf blower, a table saw with a blade that cost forty dollars. He didn't want to have to haul away the leftover lumber and construction supplies from fixing up the house, so if I took *everything* he would throw in the expensive items for free. I had all the enthusiasm of a new parent unaware of the horrors he was wading into and barely enough furniture to fill one room, so I took it all. Two dozen patio pavers and leftover wood trim along with a one-hundred-fifty-dollar chop saw. I didn't really have a need for a chop saw, but maybe it would motivate me to finally start up that side hustle making woodblock prints of newborn fawns and garden gnomes.

I didn't entirely mind slipping into this life-in-progress. It was easier picking up where the previous owner had left off than confronting the loneliness I felt buying a house alone. All I needed to do was take on this already constructed persona left for me, this skin I could try on and walk around in for a while until I figured out what or who I wanted to be.

∼

Growing up, I wanted to be Pee-wee Herman.

To me, Pee-wee seemed like the perfect blend of child and adult. He was funny and charming and kind to his friends and neighbors when they stopped by to chat or gossip. He was wise and always seemed to come up with creative solutions to problems. He knew how to entertain himself, but he also had an adventurous streak. At the end of each episode of *Pee-wee's Playhouse*, he hopped on his bicycle and pedaled off in search of adventure, as I often imagined myself doing, zipping away from my family's farm on my Huffy.

My favorite scenes of *Pee-wee's Playhouse* were the ones where everyone got together at the playhouse, like when Pee-wee can't decide who to take to dinner so Jambi helps him throw a luau or when Pee-wee puts on a magic show and everyone shows up (including hunky, shirtless lifeguard Tito in a gold bow tie and matching trunks). I especially loved the scene from the pilot episode where Pee-wee invites everyone to the playhouse for a pool party. When the rain moves everyone inside, Pee-wee gets to play the gracious host by making ice cream soup. (It's just melted ice cream with a few pumps of chocolate syrup.) It doesn't really matter that the rain has ruined the pool party. What matters is that everyone is there—Cowboy Curtis, Miss Yvonne, Nosy neighbor Mrs. Steve, Tito, The Playhouse Gang (Opal, Elvis, and Cher)— and that they are all focused on Pee-wee.

I thought owning a house would make me feel more connected with other people. It would show everyone that I was committed to the community and that I cared about my neighbors. I would no longer be this transient wanderer jumping from apartment to apartment and community to community. With a house, I could open up and show everyone I cared. I would be like Pee-wee: kind and generous and always there.

～

My house was in an unfamiliar city where I didn't know anyone, so between painting rooms and unboxing books and kitchen appliances, I obsessively checked Grindr and OkCupid for messages from strangers, for some recognition that I was being seen, for *something* to combat the loneliness at the intersection of ending a relationship and buying a house alone. It didn't help that it was winter in Minnesota, and the snow and ice made me feel numb and empty inside.

To fill the void, I invited the men I met on the apps to my house. I invited them to hang out, to watch TV, to talk about their lives, but we usually did more than that. Often, we found our way to my bedroom

where I pulled their bodies toward mine, feeling their heat, their weight.
I kissed their lips and necks and clavicles. I gripped their biceps, placed
my palms against their chests, grabbed their hips and pulled them closer.
I didn't care if my aggressiveness turned them off. I just kept reaching
for them so they wouldn't forget that I was there.

These encounters helped me feel better, but those feelings were
fleeting. I still felt somewhat invisible living in that house alone, in the
dead of winter, surrounded by these silent neighbors I had yet to meet.
None of those random hookups helped me shake that hollow feeling
that I was utterly alone. One guy pointed to my bedroom window, which
I had yet to cover with a curtain, and asked whether I was concerned
that my neighbors might see what we were doing.

"Don't worry," I assured the man as I reached for his belt buckle.
"No one really even knows I'm here."

~

Three weeks into living in my house, someone dumped a car with
busted-out windows on the shared pavement between my neighbor's
garage and mine. I noticed it there early one afternoon when I looked
out the office window overlooking my backyard. It was snowing gently,
and I watched as the snow landed on the car and fell into the back seat.
If that car hadn't been there, I would have found it serene. Instead, I
found the whole thing eerie—this abandoned car slowly disappearing
under the snow. I wasn't sure what to do. I had nowhere to go that day,
but I was worried the car would still be there in the morning when I
needed to drive to work. Eventually, after hours of watching the car, I
walked next door and knocked on my neighbor's door.

An old man answered, and before I could introduce myself and explain the situation, he blurted out, "Call the police! Call the police!" I
just nodded and walked back to my house.

After the police hauled the car away, another neighbor explained that
this had happened before—the dumping of an unwanted car near our
neighbor's house—and that it was a gang thing, where an abandoned
car with busted-out windows was some kind of threat. I heard my

neighbor's explanation, but I wasn't really listening. I was too busy star-ing at the snowless patch where the car had been parked and thinking about how nicely snow covers what we hope to ignore.

I wanted to ignore that lonely feeling of my life being in flux—this period of readjustment where everything was so static and still—and the best way to do that was to adopt a different way of being. When I bought my house, I thought I would feel better, more complete or more adjusted or more whole in some way. But I didn't feel anything standing next to my garage, staring at that empty space where the car had been parked. I felt like no one. I felt hollow and cold and numb. I'd been hiding in my house, being someone that wasn't really me and pretending to live this alternative life because I was scared that I would never be able to readjust and turn my life into what I wanted it to be. It seemed entirely possible that I would forever live in this purgatory January, stuck between what I used to be and what I wanted to become. The month would just keep playing over and over—same dark corners, same faceless men, same empty spaces—until I figured out who I was supposed to be.

I went inside and let the snow blanket everything: the pavement where the car had been, the yard where I was planning to plant peren-nials and vegetables, the house where I continued to hide. I let the snow continue to bury me so that, when I was ready, I could crawl out from under it and try again.

Chameleon Boy

Between the wooden slats of the bookshelf in my living room, I see Donald Trump on the back cover of a comic book. He is crouched in the lower corner, an intruder poised at the edge of my life. I first noticed him a few nights ago—creeping, watching—and now I imagine him lurking in other places around my house. I imagine him in the bathroom, his scowling face peeking out from inside the tub. Behind the toaster, in the onion patch, tucked inside my sock drawer. I imagine him smirking while watching me sleep.

I tell this to my boyfriend, Matt. It is his bookshelf, his book.

"This guy?" he says, pointing at the Trump look-alike. "He's not even human."

It doesn't matter whether the figure is human or not. I know the figure isn't *supposed* to look like Trump, but that is what I see, and what matters to me now is that Matt sees Trump, too.

I've been thinking a lot about permanence lately, how moving things become still, remain, shift into something else. This bookshelf is in my first house—my first real home after years of moving around—and Matt is the first boyfriend I've ever asked to move in with me. It feels very concrete, very settled. But also very raw, all the jagged edges of our new relationship rough and ready to harm. I worry that he won't like it here, that I won't like *him* here. I worry that he'll get bored. I worry about change—him changing me, me changing him, neither of us changing at all. Mostly, I worry about not seeing eye to eye.

"Chameleon Boy," Matt says about the Trump look-alike. "From the Legion of Super-Heroes."

I know nothing about Chameleon Boy, so when he says this, I imagine a half-lizard, half-boy creature with the ability to morph into just about anything—a bird, a rocket, a billionaire with an unnatural-looking comb-over. I imagine a superhero constantly changing, never still, someone who easily blends into his surroundings. I picture a character like X-Men's Nightcrawler, a creature I emulated in my twenties with my constant moving, my nonstop wanderlust. Job to job. Place to place. Boyfriend to boyfriend. I never stayed with anything for longer than two years. I morphed, changed, moved on when the camouflage wore off, when I realized I would probably never really fit in.

"Yeah, but doesn't he look like Trump to you?" I ask. "Don't you see it?"

I think about those ambiguous images I saw when I was a child, the ones where some people see one thing and others see something else. Once, our teacher showed us a black-and-white figure and asked us what we saw. My classmates said they saw a young woman. I stared at the figure until I saw the woman too—her feathered hat and billowy veil and furry coat. Then, our teacher asked, *Do you see the old woman?* I squinted hard at the figure. All I saw was the young woman, her single eyelash and small nose turned away. I tried to see an old woman in the figure, but I couldn't make my eyes see what I wanted them to see. Instead of raising my hand and asking the teacher to point it out, I pretended I saw the old woman because my classmates said they saw her and I didn't want to be left out.

Now, I want Matt to see Trump on the comic book so I can know that our relationship will work out, that I've made the right choice in asking him to live with me, that I belong in this house with him. But Matt doesn't see what I see. He sees Chameleon Boy and only Chameleon Boy, and instead of thinking our relationship is doomed and that I should run away as I've always done before, I just smile back at him and try to imagine the hazy space between being one thing and being something else—that middle ground where everything seems to float or flutter or vibrate because it doesn't know which direction it should go. *Is it a young woman looking away? A shape-shifting alien? Or is it something else, something blurry and obscure, something difficult to define and pin down, something never still?*

Later, I'll ask Matt questions about the characters in the comic books he reads in bed—Animal Man, Ragman, the Creeper; so many men pretending to be something else—and we'll argue about the meaning of the term *secret identity*. He'll say that it refers to a superhero's civilian identity, when he isn't assuming his superhero persona, and I'll disagree. I'll argue that superheroes are civilians *first*. Then they become something more, take on alter egos, shift into other identities. The superhero identities *are* the secret identities, hidden from others, not the other way around.

Matt will laugh, shake his head. He wouldn't hesitate to tell me I'm wrong.

Breathe In

Walking up to the Minneapolis VA hospital for the first time, I feel a long-forgotten sense of dread and shame. I've been out of the military for fifteen years, and I'm not in uniform, but it's the same feeling that I used to get walking up to any chow hall or military building on the Balad Air Base in Iraq. Dread because I hated always having to be on guard and alert in case I passed an officer and needed to salute. Shame because often I'd be thinking about something else, pass an officer without saluting, and then get called out by the officer for not respecting rank and not paying attention to my demeanor or my surroundings. Once, outside the PX, the makeshift store where we bought junk food and deodorant and CDs, an officer yelled at me for several minutes while I stood in a position of attention and tried to imagine what would happen if I just took off in a dead sprint away from him.

I am early for my appointment, so I spend ten minutes just wandering the halls. I find the chapel and the cafeteria, the emergency department and a lobby of people waiting for x-rays. I pass a woman who can't find her husband. Another woman is knocking on the door to the single-user restroom, asking whether *her* husband is in there. He is not, but someone else is. On my way back toward the main entrance, I pass a couple just as the wife turns to her husband and tells him to use the restroom while she pulls the car around. I smile at both of them, but they don't notice me at all.

I am at the VA to participate in a research study called "Service and Health among Deployed Veterans" (SHADE). The purpose of the study is to learn more about the long-term impact of deployments on the health of veterans who served in Iraq, Kuwait, Djibouti, Kyrgyzstan, Afghanistan, and Qatar after October 1, 2001. For years, I'd been reading reports and news stories of veterans coming down with a whole range of unexplainable symptoms after serving overseas. Veterans contracting sinusitis or asthma or getting ulcers or open lesions on their skin. Vets who were perfectly healthy before being deployed but returned barely able to exercise without getting winded. Vets dying of rare cancers or contracting respiratory illnesses like chronic obstructive pulmonary disease, which causes coughing and wheezing and makes it difficult to breathe. Some vets started to point to the open pits used to burn trash on military bases as the culprit of these ailments. But when they filed claims for treatment and disability benefits with the VA, they were denied because of the lack of proof that burn pits were making them sick. Additionally, it took years for some of these symptoms to even materialize, forcing some vets to wait for approval for their claims before they could even set up appointments with the VA. People started calling burn pits my generation's Agent Orange.

Reading all this information about burn pits over the years, I started to wonder whether my own mysterious ailments were connected to my time in Iraq. When I started getting headaches on a regular basis in graduate school and was told it was just stress, I thought about the burn pit I had served near and the smoke I'd seen wafting from it. When my sinuses started flaring up, I wondered whether something I had been exposed to gave me chronic sinusitis or something worse. I had a CT scan done on my ribs and was told I had a fatty, benign tumor— nothing to worry about, but still uncommon for a twenty-six-year-old. I couldn't help but blame my military service. Part of me wanted to believe that these concerns were psychological, my mind jumping to the easiest conclusion. But another part of me worried that it was something more than that, that my paranoia was valid and real. Then, a friend posted a new story about her childhood friend, a Minnesota National Guard veteran named Amie Muller, who had served in Iraq in 2005 and 2007 and who died at thirty-six, nine months after being diagnosed with Stage III pancreatic cancer, ten years after she returned home. Muller believed she had gotten sick from exposure to the open burn pit at Balad Air Base, the same base I'd served at from 2003 to 2004. I didn't know Muller, but I knew the place she had been. Reading about her made the controversy feel closer than ever before. It felt real.

Just inside the VA's main entrance, I locate the clinic where I need to be and check in at the receptionist's desk. After about five minutes of waiting, I look up and see a young woman step out from behind the front desk and call my name. She introduces herself as Maddy, shakes my hand, and asks me about the weather as she leads me down the hall. She doesn't have a lab coat or a clipboard. We don't enter a fancy conference room with recording equipment, potted plants, and natural light pouring in through the blinds—my vision of where a government-funded scientific study might take place. We step into a small, windowless room with a computer and a couple chairs and a tiny sink in the corner with a clock above it displaying the wrong time.

I sit in the chair against the wall and clamp my hands between my knees to stop them from shaking. We go through the consent form together, and then, after recording my height, weight, and pulse, Maddy starts asking me about my military history. She wants to know where I served and how long I was there. I tell her about Balad Air Base, where I spent most of my time while I was in Iraq. She types this into the computer, then looks over at me and asks the question I've been expecting.

"Was there a burn pit there?"

～

We called it The Dump. It was in the northwest corner of Balad Air Base. When I first arrived at Balad in May 2003, near the beginning of the American occupation of Iraq, The Dump was little more than a growing mound of trash. As the weeks went on and the number of troops at Balad Air Base grew, so did The Dump. By December of that year, the single mound had grown to become a maze of heaps set aflame. The Dump would eventually grow to span more than ten acres and burn more than two hundred tons of trash a day.

One day that December I was tasked with escorting a group of Iraqi laborers to The Dump to repair a section of the perimeter fencing. Someone had been hiring kids to crawl under the fence and steal some of the more valuable items from The Dump, and a soldier at a guard station had shot one of the kids in the leg. My job was to supervise the workers and make sure they did a good job, so that no more kids got shot. It seemed like a cruel trick to ask the Iraqi people to fix a problem the U.S. military had created, but it wasn't my job to question it. I just nodded when the sergeant in charge gave me my orders.

After the workers finished patching up the fence, they took to scavenging through the trash in The Dump and making piles of items they wanted to take with them. They brought back Christmas wreaths and old truck tires and empty powdered-Gatorade tubs. They carried over broken box fans and aluminum cans and even photographs they found mixed in with everything else. They wanted so many of the things we had just tossed away. Watching them make their piles of our trash, I felt embarrassed by all the waste we produced, how we could toss away so much when many of the Iraqi people outside the base had so little. I'd like to say that I thought twice about all the unnecessary things I bought at the PX after seeing this, but I'm sure that isn't true. I still bought CDs and junk food and magazines that eventually ended up in The Dump.

When it came time to tell the workers that they couldn't take any of the trash from The Dump, I asked one of the other soldiers to do it. I didn't have the heart to tell the workers that the treasures they'd found were all supposed to be burned.

At the time, I didn't recognize how much of an impact The Dump had on the rest of the base. The lot next to our tents was covered in this finely ground sand—powder, really. It was unlike any sand I'd seen before. Every time a vehicle left the motor pool, where we parked our Humvees and trucks, it kicked up clouds of dust that wafted over the tents where we slept. I'd find the sand in my boots, inside the folds of my sleeping bag, in between my toes and in the crooks of my arms. During the summer, when we slept with the tent flaps rolled up, I'd wake to find a fine layer covering every inch of my sleeping area. I would joke to the other members of my platoon that the sand was burying us alive. I found this genuinely funny at the time.

"It's like walking through ash," Danny, a member of my platoon, said once, as we kicked our way across the motor pool. Danny found the sand interesting. He had taken to collecting it in miniature Tabasco sauce bottles that came in the MRE (Meal, Ready-to-Eat) packets. He showed me four tiny bottles in the palm of his hand. I pinched one between my thumb and forefinger and stared at the sand inside. I admitted to him that I was also a little mesmerized by the sand, but I didn't tell him that I'd taken to picking up handfuls and letting the grains fall between my fingers as I walked across the motor pool, just for the sensation of feeling the powder against my skin. It made me feel light and carefree, as if even I could float away at any minute.

Not once did it cross my mind that the sand might have been ash from the burn pits at The Dump. I just assumed that the sand in Iraq was different. This ancient Babylonian sand ground to powder from years of being trod upon.

It wasn't until after I returned from Iraq that I found out what all was tossed into those burn pits at The Dump. Plastics, Styrofoam, paint, chemical waste, unexploded ordnance, used needles. Even amputated limbs. It was all soaked in diesel fuel and lit on fire, and from those fires pollutants, including benzene, dioxin, and other carcinogens, were released into the air and carried across the base. We breathed in these pollutants walking to the chow hall. We breathed them in while driving around base. We breathed them in while standing guard, while staring at all that ashy sand, while dreaming about our families and friends, while thinking about going home.

∼

When I was five, my father was burning trash in the center of our farm, and fire escaped the burn-barrel and leaped across the yard. The fire burned the tall grasses near our house and the brambles and young trees in one of our sheep pens. Our local fire department was called, and while they put out the fire, I waited inside our house and watched my mother cry. I wanted to look out the window, to see what the fire was destroying, but I couldn't look away from my mother. She was afraid that the fire would take away everything she and my father had worked so hard to create. She had no real way of knowing what would be destroyed.

The fire didn't cause any major damage; just enough for us to notice. In the days after the fire, I walked around the scorched yard and examined what had been ravaged. I walked over all the charred grass. I ran my hand over the blackened baseboards of one of our outbuildings, the one half-full of junk. I stopped in front of what used to be a beautiful, mature green ash tree with two trunks. The fire had burned away the branches and licked out the insides of one of the trunks. I stuck my hand inside and wiggled it around. There was nothing there. It was hollow, just a husk. But the other trunk of the tree survived. In the years after the fire, it continued to grow branches and leaves, while the destroyed trunk remained a blackened shell.

I hated seeing the tree like that, half of what it used to be. But something about its transformation mesmerized me. As a bookish kid, I knew what I was supposed to see in that half-destroyed tree. Perseverance. Rebirth. Beauty in the scarred. I didn't really see any of that. Instead, I stared at the two halves and wondered about the power of fire, how some things get caught in the flames while others escape seemingly unscathed.

~

I keep thinking about how risky it can be to simply do a job, about all these hazards that come with mere work. Fire and fumes and toxic mold. IEDs and stray bullets and dust. I think about the jobs I've had—paperboy, janitor, farmhand—and all the different ways those jobs could have killed me. Getting run over one dark morning while tossing a newspaper onto a stoop. Slipping on a newly waxed floor. Being dragged behind a wild horse while out tending to the land. (That actually happened to one of my distant relatives.) There are so many ways to die while working.

I was twenty-two when I arrived in Iraq, young and naïve and unsure of so many of my abilities as a soldier. Soon after being deployed, I figured out that the easiest thing to do was to surrender my body to the Army as completely as I could. I listened to the sergeants and officers who told me what to do, where to be, and how to act. I saluted them when I noticed them on the base and stayed on guard for when I might need to do so again. I listened when the staff sergeant talked about IEDs and the enemies beyond the wire that was trying to harm me just for being an American soldier. And I knew enough about "friendly fire" to know that I could die at the hands of the soldiers I was serving with. For the most part, the media and my military training prepared me for what to expect in Iraq.

It's the unforeseen hazards, the dangers I couldn't predict, that haunt me now. Every time I read another story about a 9/11 first responder dying from some cancer linked to the World Trade Center collapsing— like the burn pits, it had been doused in jet fuel and set alight—I think about how my own naive trust in the military overpowered my concerns about the occupational hazards associated with doing my job. I was too young and too naïve to imagine the risks that come with living and working near a burn pit, let alone the harm the burn pits did to the bodies of Iraqis who lived nearby. It wasn't in the media; it wasn't in my military training. If I had known, I might have thought twice about marching through all that dust and smoke without a mask and scooping up handfuls of that ashy sand. Maybe I would have paused a little bit before so completely surrendering my body to an organization that talked a good talk but, ultimately, saw me the same way it saw everyone else, my fellow soldiers and the Iraqis who surrounded us: as disposable.

~

Maddy hands me an information sheet about the VA's Airborne Hazards & Open Burn Pit Registry. I already know about the Registry. I'd heard about it in 2014, when it was first created for service members to document exposures and report health concerns, but I had put off completing the questionnaire for the Registry for five years because I was afraid of going down an unhealthy path of obsession. There was still so much unknown about the effects of exposure to burn pits, and I didn't want speculation to take over my life and lead to a quest for someone or something to blame. Plus, I didn't fully trust that the military would make things right.

If I didn't complete the questionnaire, I thought, I could remain oblivious to the effects of the burn pits and avoid years of anxiety from thinking I'd been affected by living near one. To register something is to know it, to comprehend it, to notice something about it, and I wasn't sure I was ready to start noticing just yet.

But something changed over time. I couldn't easily avoid burn pits, even if I wanted to. I kept hearing about them. More stories of soldiers getting sick. News articles about advancing research on chronic respiratory illnesses. Not-yet-president Joe Biden acknowledging the link between burn pits and his son Beau's death from brain cancer in 2015. Jon Stewart signing onto advocacy efforts to raise awareness about illnesses related to burn pit exposure. Finally, in 2019, before my visit to the VA, I consented and sat down in front of my computer to complete the Registry's questionnaire. For a while I just stared at the number of people who'd registered before me—180,750—and read the factoids on the website. Eventually, I clicked on the questionnaire's link, took a deep breath in, and started answering questions.

The questionnaire asked about location specific exposures in Iraq and Kuwait, whether I was involved in trash hauling or burning, whether I knew who ran the burn pits and how many hours a day smoke or fumes from burn pits entered my work or housing site. I don't remember the smoke being distracting or so thick I couldn't see, but I remember often walking across our company's section of base and seeing little fires everywhere. There were fires in common areas outside a cluster of tents. There were fires outside the outhouses we built because we had to burn our own shit and piss. I would often look up and, if the sky was clear, see smoke drifting up from somewhere off base, wafting up from the horizon and drifting over our tents while we slept. Thinking about it now, it seemed perfectly normal to see smoke every day in Iraq. Smoke was everywhere. But why was that?

The questionnaire tried to get me to think of other exposures to airborne hazards, too, things outside Iraq. It asked where I had lived the longest before I was thirteen, which got me thinking about the trash barrel on the farm I grew up on and everything we burned in it. It asked whether I'd smoked more than one hundred cigarettes in my lifetime (I haven't, but I thought about how other people answered this. Was this just something you knew? Or did people actually spend time counting their cigarettes consumed?). It asked whether I'd ever removed mold from my home (I hadn't), whether there were any "traditional farm animals" on land where I lived or visited (there weren't), and whether I participated in any hobbies such as woodworking, welding, pottery, or "hobbies utilizing epoxy resin adhesives" (I don't). I knew these questions were meant to get a "whole picture" of the possible ways I could have been exposed to airborne toxins, but I wondered whether they were just distracting me from thinking about burn pits. I wondered whether the creators of the questionnaire knew that people would automatically come to the questionnaire suspicious about burn pits, so they needed to shift their attention elsewhere.

The entire time I was completing the questionnaire my left lung— the one I'd had a CT scan on many years earlier—lightly ached and throbbed.

~

Even after claims about the dangers of burn pits started surfacing, the U.S. Department of Defense continued to use them overseas. They claimed that incinerators were just too costly to operate overseas, that there was no good alternative to burn pits. They claimed that open burn pits were the best way to reduce waste and protect service members.

I don't think about protection when I think about burn pits. I think about luck and ashy sand and falling into a deep, bottomless abyss. I think about uncertainty and the tree trunk scooped out by fire and all the different ways we catalogue and record how trauma can hollow out those it touches, like the Holocaust survivors and victims' registries and the registries created after the World Trade Center collapsed. Mostly, I think about how all the controversy with burn pits could have been avoided if there had been more regulations in place about what could and could not be burned, if American troops weren't thought of as expendable, if there had been more sensitivity to how we damage the environment and how the environment can damage us back.

Sometimes, when I read about burn pits now, I catch myself holding my breath in anticipation. I'm not sure what I'm waiting for. Maybe for the research to speed up or some missing piece of information explicitly linking burn pit exposure to specific illnesses and conditions or maybe some magic remedy to ease the anxiety associated with waiting to get sick. Really, I just want more accountability. I want the military to more explicitly acknowledge the mishandling of burn pits that killed and harmed so many men and women, both military and civilian. I don't expect to get this anytime soon, so while I wait, I'll keep reading about burn pits and sharing stories of veterans getting sick and holding my breath, waiting for the day to let all that air out.

~

The final part of my appointment is a breathing test to measure my lung function. I am to take a deep breath in and then exhale as hard as I can into the spirometer, which is connected to Maddy's computer. Maddy pretends to put the spirometer into her mouth and demonstrates what I should do before handing it over to me.

I put a nose clip in place and insert the spirometer into my mouth. I sit back into my chair, back stiff and as upright as I possibly can. Then I nod at Maddy, take a deep breath in through my mouth, and push that air out as fast and as hard as I can.

"Keep going, keep going, almost there," Maddy says, watching the program on her computer record my breathing.

I wait for Maddy to give me the *all clear*, then remove the spirometer from my mouth and the clip from my nose and cough into my sleeve.

"How was that?" Maddy asks.

I sit back in my chair and look over at her.

"Fine," I say. "Just fine."

I can't tell if Maddy thinks my breathing is normal or if she already detects something is wrong with me when she compares my data to those of other vets she's interviewed. I want to ask her about all the other men and women. I don't talk to the men and women I served with anymore, and now I'm finding that I wish I had stayed in touch with them, so I could ask if anyone else was feeling this anxiety about burn pits, if anyone else couldn't stop thinking about them. But I don't. I just smile at Maddy when she tells me to take a minute to compose myself before I breathe into the spirometer again.

I do the breathing test three more times, coughing into my sleeve after each test. Then, Maddy takes the spirometer and inserts a canister of albuterol, which is supposed to open up my airways. I take two puffs of albuterol, and after thirty minutes we perform the breathing test again. I don't feel a difference as I push the air out of my lungs.

I will receive the results of the breathing test a few weeks later, in the form of a letter from one of the researchers. My breathing is normal, nothing to worry about and no better after using albuterol. I'll stare at the letter for a few minutes, wondering how useful this new information is, how truthful this information really is, before filing it away with all the other stories and reports and research about burn pits.

At the end of the appointment, Maddy tells me about other studies being conducted on veterans' health and an email listserv that sends updates about the SHADE study. I thank her as she walks me to the door, then shake her hand and step out into a hallway. I don't talk to anyone as I walk to the main entrance. Instead, I keep my head down and slip out into the January sunshine, past the security guards manning the entrance, the wives looking for their wandering husbands, the vets in wheelchairs waiting for their rides. I escape back into the world undetected. Burn pits haven't gotten me yet.

A New State of Being

During the first meeting between my parents and the man who would become my husband, my mother told a story from my childhood that had me wondering whether I had finished playing the role of the "wandering son."

We were at a restaurant in St. Paul—me; my boyfriend, Matt; and my parents. Matt and I had been dating for about six months, living together for less than three, and we were still peeling back our layers and revealing our histories to each other bit by bit. I was still a little restless, feeling the pull of other places but also feeling the need to be still, to stand for a little while in one place and see what accumulated around me.

"Once, I lost Bronson," my mother said, beginning her favorite story about me. "We were farming a couple of miles from the house, and he was a toddler. Just old enough to walk."

I shook my head as my mother began this story. I'd heard this story a million times, and every time I heard it, I wondered why my mother told it. There were millions of stories she could have told. Why this one?

"I turned around and he wasn't there," my mother continued. "He was gone. Nowhere in sight. I started running down the pasture, toward the farm, looking for him and yelling his name."

When my mother said this, I pictured her feathered hair blown back by the breeze as she ran. I pictured her wearing a puffy vest, jeans, this frantic look on her face. She was thin and hopeful and alive. She wasn't burdened by six children or broken-down vehicles or trying to scrape together a living on the North Dakota prairie.

"Then I saw him, waddling back and forth, making his way toward the milkhouse," she said. "When I got to him, he was saying *milk, milk, milk* over and over and over."

I let my mother get away with this exaggeration because it wasn't too far off from the toddler I imagined I was—this happy infant tottering across the prairie grass, desperately trying to find his way to the thing he loved most. I also thought that, unbeknownst to my mother, the story depicted the man I'd become—often annoyingly jovial, unburdened, continuously on the move. My mother's always-wandering son.

But something about the depiction didn't sit right with me. It wasn't that my mother's depiction of me was false. It was more that I wanted something else to be true.

I didn't want to be that wandering son anymore.

∼

At Christmas a few months earlier, I looked around the room—at my four younger brothers and their wives and their children—and realized how out of place I was among my family. My siblings had all stayed close to my parents. Some of them never left the state. They had inside jokes and stories and things I wasn't a part of because I'd wandered away from all of them. I was the one who joined the military and fell in love with traveling and lived in China for two years, the one who kept all the details about his personal life hazy and unspecific, the one who spent years constructing another version of himself to cover up his rural, Midwestern upbringing. Watching the way my brothers interacted with one another, I wondered whether my family even really knew me anymore. Did they know anything about the man I'd become? Did anyone?

∼

The first time I invited Matt over to my house, I cooked sesame-spiced meatballs and chickpea salad with lemon and sumac. I'd recently bought a cookbook and had decided that after all those years of wandering and moving around I was finally going to start learning to cook for myself, at the age of thirty-two. I collected the breadcrumbs and sesame seeds and chickpeas from the local supermarket and then made a special trip to a spice store for Aleppo pepper and ground sumac. I had never prepared chickpeas or even known what ground sumac was, but I recognized learning to cook as the next logical step in my evolution from a shiftless son into a stable, home-owning adult. I wanted to show myself as a provider, someone who knew how to take care of others, someone who wasn't just concerned with himself. I was finally ready to live for more than just myself.

It wasn't long after that first date that I asked Matt to move in with me, the first boyfriend I'd ever asked. I had never stayed in one place long enough to make it to that moment. There had been boyfriends who had *wanted* to take the next step with me, who were waiting for me to ask them about living together, but I just wasn't ready or interested enough in making that commitment. Living together seemed like such an intimate act, and for much of my twenties I was just too immature to make that jump, too wild and independent to be tied down.

I spent those first few months living with Matt getting used to his presence, learning what it felt like to orbit so closely around another human being. I treaded lightly, unsure of my movements, unsure of making the wrong move or of having Matt see something that I didn't want him to see. I didn't want him to see the man I had fashioned myself into during my twenties, the one who let wanderlust direct his every move. I wanted him to see a different person, one who wasn't afraid of letting people in, one who didn't keep everyone at arm's length. I wanted to show him this new man I was becoming, this version of myself that wasn't so flighty and selfish and distant.

$\sim$

When I explained these first few months of my relationship with Matt to my friend Yuko, she described it as a "new state of being." I had stepped from my previous state as a wandering son to this new plane of existence. In this new state, I slowed down, thought about how my actions impacted others, learned to open up and not keep everyone and everything at a distance. I didn't necessarily feel like a different person or as if I were putting on a persona of someone else. I felt that I was building a new version of myself that had never before been constructed. A version that had until now existed only in my dreams.

In this new state of being, the neighborhood around me came alive. I had spent so little time stationary in the past that I had never gotten to know my neighbors and my neighborhood. I took long walks through the neighborhood with my pug, stopping often to admire the wild ways nature sprang up before me or the careful attempts my neighbors had made at keeping up appearances. I noticed when certain trees were in bloom, the days when the neighborhood kids would gather in the park to play soccer, the ways my neighbors sauntered down the sidewalk. The elderly couple who lived next door kept to themselves, but I often saw the man in his backyard playing the qeej—a Hmong musical organ made from bamboo. Sometimes he gave lessons to children and adults in the neighborhood. The old woman who lived across the alley often stood on her back stoop late in the afternoons, staring off into the middle distance while her French bulldog relieved himself in her yard.

That first spring, I was standing before the garden beds planning out what would go where—kale in the front, tomatoes in the back, zucchini along the edge so the vines could snake off the side—when my neighbor two doors down waved from across his yard.

"What kind of rock do you have there?" he asked, pointing at the dark stone along the side of my house.

I leaned into the chain link fence and looked at him across our in-between neighbor's yard.

"Some kind of shale, I think," I replied and then invited him over to take a look.

Standing in my yard, he introduced himself as Vone and welcomed me to the neighborhood. We shook hands. Then, Vone reached down and took a handful of the shale and let it fall slowly through his fingers. We talked about the neighborhood and our houses and all the projects we had planned out as homeowners. He was friendly, easy to talk to, the kind of neighbor I'd always heard about, one who'd gladly lend you a ladder or help you fix a busted pipe.

A few weeks later, I was walking my pug down the alley when Frank, a neighbor who lived across the alley from Vone, waved me over and asked whether I'd heard about Vone. I shook my head.

"He was murdered," Frank said.

When I got back to my house, I looked it up online and discovered that an angry patron had shot Vone over a twenty-dollar pool tab. Vone's wife—pregnant with their fifth child—was waiting in the car outside the bar they owned to give him a ride home.

The wake at Vone's house lasted several days. A tent was erected over the back deck, and large pots were set over camping stoves. Women arrived with plates of food, and men lugged coolers up onto the deck and handed around beer. Children ran around the side yard laughing and yelling. In the evenings, people sat under the tent smoking and drinking and playing cards.

I watched this all from my deck and thought about how loved and cherished and integral Vone was to this community. I had never felt a kind of kinship with a neighbor before, and watching friends and family and community members come and go from the wake made me long for that kind of connection, where I felt part of this larger being. I hadn't felt that way since my time in the military. Maybe, now that I'd settled down a little bit, this kind of connection could be possible.

Vone's house sat empty for several months after the wake. Vone's wife installed automatic lights to make any potential intruders believe someone was living there. Occasionally, I saw her pull up behind the house and rush inside. She often came back to her car with a few items— pillows or picture frames or a lamp or two—before hopping in her car and driving away. I couldn't blame her for not wanting to live in the house anymore. I'm sure there were too many memories of an incomplete life there, too many ghosts still lurking around.

Often that fall, I was out in my backyard with my pug when the automatic lights came on. The house would be dark and ominous, and then the lights would blink on, all at once, as if the house were suddenly powering up. For a while I would just stare at the glowing house, mesmerized by its brightness, thinking about Vone and his family and how lonely and separated Vone's wake made me feel. Then I'd blink, shake away my dreaming, and vow to do something about the pangs I felt deep in my stomach.

~

We sold my first house and bought a different one, in a different neighborhood in the same city. It was a couple of years after my parents met Matt, and we were at the brewery down the street—me, my parents, and Matt—playing "Do You Remember?," a game where we tried to stump each other by recalling incidents from my childhood. For some reason, the most memorable incidents were all accidents.

"Do you remember the time Nikki got hit in the face with a basketball and broke her Coke-bottle glasses?" I asked my mother.

My mother set down her beer and smiled.

"She came running into the house bawling," she said.

My parents couldn't afford to buy her new glasses, so they just taped the old ones up, which made my brothers and me tease her even more.

"I remember the time Bo followed us on our bikes down the horse trail and how he veered off and crashed into a piece of farm equipment," I said. "Do you remember that?"

Again, my mother nodded. I was having a hard time stumping her.

"Do you remember the time you walked back to the farm in search of milk?" my father asked. "You were still a baby."

I laughed a little and nodded.

"How could I forget that one?" I said. "Mom tells it all the time."

To this, my mother lifted her beer glass and clanked it against mine.

My parents sold the farm shortly after I graduated from high school and left for college. I was off wandering when they auctioned off all the farm equipment and land, so I didn't get to walk around and reminisce about growing up there. Instead, I heard about the auction from my family, and during the years after the sale, I heard stories about how the man who bought the farm had changed it.

"He tore down the milkhouse," my father had said earlier in my parents' visit.

The milkhouse was the first thing my parents built after buying the farm in 1979, the year before I was born, the year my older sister was born and died. When my father told me that the milkhouse was gone, I thought about the sour smells from when it used to store milk and the hollow sound the milking tank made when I tapped it and how, in the winter, the room was always warmer than anywhere else on the farm because my father kept space heaters going so the pipes wouldn't freeze.

"What did he do with the steel milk tank?" I asked after my father told me about the milk-house.

My father shrugged. He didn't know.

I pictured the blank wall of the barn where the milkhouse used to be, how awkward and bare it must have looked. This lasted only a few seconds before my mind started reconstructing the milkhouse from my childhood. I put back the walls and the window and the door. I put back the giant steel tank in the middle of the room. I put back the milkers and the tubing and everything else needed for milking. Finally, I put back myself—the waddling toddler from my mother's story, the son who'd wandered away yet found his way back, who was once again making his way across the prairie, this time creating a new story about the man he'd become. The man he wanted to be.

Acknowledgments

I'd like to thank the editors of the following publications in which these essays first appeared, often in slightly different form:

"Withers" in *Big Muddy*
"Battle Buddy" in *The Southeast Review*
"How to Reintegrate" in *Creative Nonfiction*
"Stalactites" in *Neon Door*
"You Think I'm a Boy" in *Permafrost*
"Finish Line" in *Avidly*
"Thirst & Trap" in *Hobart*
"Chameleon Boy" in *Queer Voices: Prose, Poetry & Pride*
"Breathe In" in *Guernica*

The information on gender and pronouns in the essay "You Think I'm a Boy" came from two sources: "'Diversifying' Masculinity: Super Girls, Happy Boys, Cross-Dressers, and Real Men on Chinese Media," by Huike Wen, in the fall 2013 issue of *ASIANetwork Exchange* and "Covert Sexism in Mandarin Chinese," by David Moser, in *Sino-Platonic Papers*.

I would like to express my gratitude to the Virginia Center for the Creative Arts, the Minnesota State Arts Board, and the McKnight Foundation for supporting my work and providing me with time and space to work on these essays. I am also extremely grateful to the faculty at Minnesota State University Mankato for showing me what a writing community looks like and for giving me time to think and write. Finally, thank you to the faculty, staff, and students at the University of Minnesota Rochester for welcoming me into their community.

Thank you to all the friends and readers who have offered feedback on these essays and helped me work through all the weird thoughts and drafts that went into this producing this book: Yuko Taniguchi, Jeremy Anderson, Virginia Wright-Peterson, Morgan Grayce Willow, Catherine Reid Day, Katherine Hengel, Kelly Foster Lundquist, Zoe Bird, B.J. Hollars, Kris Bigalk, Richard Terrill, Lynette Reini-Grandell, Luke Rolfes, Jenny Yang Cropp, Ande Davis, and Masie Cochran.

Love and gratitude to my family for letting me be the weirdo I was always meant to be.

Finally, thank you to Matt for putting up with me and all my strange little obsessions.

Living Out

The Last Deployment: How a Gay, Hammer-Swinging Twentysomething Survived a Year in Iraq
Bronson Lemer

The Lonely Veteran's Guide to Companionship
Bronson Lemer

Eminent Maricones: Arenas, Lorca, Puig, and Me
Jaime Manrique

1001 Beds: Performances, Essays, and Travels
Tim Miller

Body Blows: Six Performances
Tim Miller

Cleopatra's Wedding Present: Travels through Syria
Robert Tewdwr Moss

The Only Way Through Is Out
Suzette Mullen

Good Night, Beloved Comrade: The Letters of Denton Welch to Eric Oliver
Edited and with an introduction by Daniel J. Murtaugh

Taboo
Boyer Rickel

Wolf Act
AJ Romriell

Men I've Never Been
Michael Sadowski

Secret Places: My Life in New York and New Guinea
Tobias Schneebaum

Wild Man
Tobias Schneebaum

Sex Talks to Girls: A Memoir
Maureen Seaton